Bob Feller's
Little Black Book
of Baseball Wisdom

Bob Feller
with
Burton Rocks

CONTEMPORARY BOOKS

Library of Congress Cataloging-in-Publication Data

Feller, Bob, 1918–
    Bob Feller's little black book of baseball wisdom / Bob Feller
with Burton Rocks.
        p.   cm.
    ISBN 0-8092-9843-0
    1. Feller, Bob, 1918–   2. Baseball players—United States—
Biography.   3. Baseball players—United States—Anecdotes.
I. Title: Little black book of baseball wisdom.   II. Rocks, Burton.
III. Title.

    GV865.F4 A29   2001
    796.357'092—dc21
    [B]

                                                    00-64482

To my wife, Anne, who is my dearest friend on earth   —Bob

To my Mom and Dad—Marlene and Dr. Lawrence Rocks   —Burton

Interior design by Nick Panos

Published by Contemporary Books
A division of NTC/Contemporary Publishing Group, Inc.
4255 West Touhy Avenue, Lincolnwood (Chicago), Illinois 60712-1975 U.S.A.
Printed in the United States of America
International Standard Book Number: 0-8092-9843-0
01 02 03 04 05 06 LB 15 14 13 12 11 10 9 8 7 6 5 4 3 2 1

Reflections on Bob Feller

I just have this picture in my mind of Bob Feller trying to throw a fastball faster than a guy could ride a motorcycle. I saw that video as a kid, and when you see that video you think to yourself, "How are you supposed to try to hit that fastball?"

When you look at his numbers, he's one of those guys who goes down in history as one of the best pitchers ever. When you hear him talk and hear him break down what he was trying to do, the one thing that really comes through, for me, is that he had a passion for what he was doing—playing baseball.

Being out there on the hill, he loved facing the hitters. He loved getting them out. When you're in a situation like I am where you've played a long time and you've had the opportunity to talk to different players from different eras, the one thing that always seems to come through for me is that they had a passion for what they were doing. That, to me, is what this game is all about—love. It's not work. It's just about going out there and doing what you love to do and trying to do it well. That's what I think about when I hear Bob Feller's name.

—SAN DIEGO PADRE TONY GWYNN

The fastest and best pitcher I ever saw during my career was Bob Feller. He had the best fastball and curve I've ever seen.

—HALL OF FAMER TED WILLIAMS

Bob Feller did as much for integration of baseball as Happy Chandler, Jackie Robinson, and Branch Rickey by playing so many exhibition games with African American players immediately after World War II.

—HALL OF FAMER MONTE IRVIN

My mother gave me permission to miss school one day, back in 1940, so I could go to Fenway Park to see Bob Feller pitch. He won the game 2–1, a 2-hit victory over Boston. He made a lasting impression with his high kick delivery, great fastball, and very good curveball.

—ROLAND HEMOND
SENIOR VICE PRESIDENT
ARIZONA DIAMONDBACKS

He had the greatest combination of fastball and curveball that I've ever seen, and he was as direct about his opinions on life as his fastball was fast.

—HALL OF FAMER RALPH KINER

He was one of the first pitchers I faced in the big leagues. They had told me about him. They called him "Blinkie" because you'd look at him and think he couldn't see you. He had that weird windup. Before and during every game he would stretch his arms. He was one of those pitchers who could pitch every day if necessary. He had a great curveball and great control for a guy who threw that hard. Some of the greatest battles were between Bob and Tommy Henrich and Bob and Joe DiMaggio. Bob had a lot of pride. He thought he could throw that fastball by them, but not those two guys. Whenever anybody asks me who the toughest pitcher was I ever faced [I say] Bob Feller.

—HALL OF FAMER PHIL "SCOOTER" RIZZUTO

Contents

Preface

Bob Feller is the paradigm of true heroism. He was the greatest pitcher of his era, having led the American League in wins six times—the equivalent today of winning six Cy Young Awards. Bob Feller also fought for our country when duty called during World War II and was equally as great as a soldier, having received six battle citations for his heroism in combat aboard the USS *Alabama*.

Bob came along in an era in which the nation desperately needed him. The year was 1936 and he was still a kid in high school in Van Meter, Iowa. Babe Ruth had ended his career; a new era of younger players such as Joe DiMaggio, Ted Williams, Phil Rizzuto, and Warren Spahn was about to start, and there was a kid who could throw a baseball faster than you could blink an eye. Bob had everything. He was intelligent. He was clean-cut. He was a phenomenal athlete ready to break out onto Wheaties boxes, and he was still a teenager. Bob Feller brought to the Cleveland Indians a charming personality and a desire to be the unparalleled best in the sport of baseball.

If you were a sportswriter at the time you couldn't have written a better story than Bob Feller's. His life was better than a motion picture. He was born in a small town outside Van Meter, Iowa, on November 13, 1918, and lived on a picturesque midwestern farm. He had a great relationship with his parents and his father was his best pal. The two often played catch together, and in time Bob knew that his dream of earning a living by playing professional baseball would become a reality.

The Indians took notice and signed him to a professional contract in 1936 at age sixteen while he was still in high school. Bob's dream had come true. It would not be long before he pitched his first professional ballgame; from there the rest is history. He compiled 266 lifetime wins, a whopping .621 lifetime winning percentage, and was elected to the National Baseball Hall of Fame in 1962 on the first ballot. His pitching career saw him lead the league six years in wins, and seven years in strikeouts, making him the original stikeout king. He threw three no-hitters and twelve one-hitters during his fabled career, and threw a ball faster than a speeding motorcycle. The fastest pitch ever clocked on a major league player is Bob's 104 mph, when he wound up on the streets of Chicago and threw his best fastball against a speeding motorcycle. The fastball won! "Rapid Robert," as he was called by his many fans across the country, had everything. He spanned generations and struck everyone out along the way. He made the cover of *Time* magazine and Wheaties cereal boxes. He had a candy bar named after him, The Bob Feller Bar. This was the baseball part of Bob Feller's life.

Then there is the patriotic Bob Feller. He is a true American hero, having enlisted and fought for our country for almost four years during World War II. Imagine what he could have accomplished on the mound if he had not spent those years serving his country. He could have easily gained another hundred wins, as he entered the war after a twenty-five win season and came back from the war immediately winning twenty-six games in 1946. However, Bob does not look at life that way, feeling it was a privilege to serve his country, with six battle citations to prove his valor. On the USS *Alabama* many young men became acquainted with young Bob in the most unique of circumstances. Even onboard ship he was a leader, getting troops into tip-top shape for combat. When World War II finished, Bob was back on the mound striking out the likes of Ted Williams and Joe DiMaggio.

After his baseball career was over, Bob continued to live at a faster-than-light pace. He made television appearances and endorsed products. He arranged travel plans for the Indians and worked with Hilton Hotels. He collected Caterpillar tractors, signed autographs, and pitched in hundreds of exhibitions. Bob also worked the booth for 1958 Mutual Game of the Day broadcasts, as well as for televised playoff and World Series games.

Today Bob is still associated with the Indians, not just as their greatest player ever, but as a sage of wisdom and advice for younger players. He instructs during spring training and attends ballgames at Jacob's Field in Cleveland. His presence in the dugout and the clubhouse helps to preserve the glory not just of the Cleveland Indians, but of a bygone era in baseball. It's Bob's pitching lore that preserves one of the greatest eras in sports history.

Bob Feller is a baseball Hall of Famer, World War II hero, husband, father, grandfather, and friend to major league baseball. From the baseball field of dreams his father built for him on the family farm in Iowa came one of the greatest players in the history of major league baseball. Here is his wisdom. Sit back, relax, and catch his best fastball if you can!

—BURTON ROCKS

We wish to acknowledge literary agent Frank Weimann for obtaining the contract for this book. We also wish to acknowledge the efforts of NTC/Contemporary Publishing and, in particular, John Nolan, Matthew Carnicelli, and Julia Anderson for their tireless efforts in putting together a fabulous book and for promoting it so well. Great job!

—BOB FELLER AND BURTON ROCKS

PART I

Good Foundations

Growing Up in Van Meter, Iowa

Home is where your youth is, where your family is, and where you grow up. My home in Iowa was three miles northeast of the town of Van Meter, and I'm proud that I grew up on that farm, in that state, and with my parents.

I enjoyed life in Van Meter, and I knew everyone in town—the barber, the grocery man, and the druggist at the pharmacy where I purchased milkshakes in the late 1920s and early 1930s. Many pharmacies in the East and the Midwest operated soda fountains that dispensed the finest milkshakes around. A strawberry sundae from the soda fountain was the best treat in the world to a kid in Van Meter.

I lived in the countryside and went to town with my father to sell the grain, corn, hogs, and livestock from our farm. We'd sell the grain at the grain elevator, buy lumber, and shop at the grocery store. On Saturday nights I'd sit in the grandstand and listen to the high school band play. Van Meter had no movie theater, but there were outdoor events in summer that kept us entertained. In winter, after a snowfall, I would take my Flexible Flyer sled, tie it to the fender of the schoolbus, and slide down the hill during lunch hours.

The Feller farm was where I could be found when school let out. I couldn't wait to get home, finish the chores, and then play catch with my dad. I was on the starting five at Van Meter High, and I played ball for my Bible school during summer vacation. The preacher at our Methodist church would bring me home, and my mother would give him some produce out of our garden or orchard.

I tried to make a baseball player out of my sister, Marguerite, but couldn't do it. She played basketball well and was on the Van Meter High girls basketball team. She was also the Iowa State Ping-Pong champion! She later became a nurse, but she was a true athlete.

I knew my teachers well, and I thought our school superintendents were great. When I graduated from high school, I left them a display case with trophies, which is still in the school. My picture hangs in the hallway. My classmates and teammates still live in Van Meter, and I'm proud of my roots there.

The Field of Dreams My Dad Built for Me

I can honestly say that I learned to play this wonderful game known to the world as baseball right in my own backyard. My first coach was my very own father. My dad did something for me that changed my entire life, and I recommend that fathers everywhere try doing it for their children. He built me my own "field of dreams" (the model upon which Kevin Costner based his movie *Field of Dreams* fifty-seven years later). Dad was ahead of his time when he built me a ballpark back in 1932.

Mother's father, Ed Ferret, had a ball diamond about two miles away on his farm in Booneville. That was what gave my father the idea to build us our own ball diamond. The concept of a field of dreams was my dad's idea, and he broached it to me. Naturally, as a child, I couldn't wait to get started helping him put up this park. We were a team in every respect. My father and mother gave me lots of time and lots of love, the two most important things that any parents can give their children.

My dad loved sports, baseball in particular, and he loved kids. There wasn't anything my dad wouldn't do for me. He bought me the best equipment he could—the best gloves, the best baseballs, the best bats. He bought me top-of-the-line uniforms.

The building of this field didn't happen overnight. It truly was an undertaking beyond all expectations. My father had to cut down, with an old-fashioned saw, twenty small trees! When I say small trees, I mean trees that weren't hundreds of years old, but rather one hundred or fifty years old. I helped him cut some of those trees down with our old crosscut saw, but the bark was thick and it was strenuous work.

We had eighty acres of timber on our property, mostly acorn oak, so we decided to call our little field of dreams "Oak View." We could wake up early in the morning, look down from our farm up on the hill, and see these beautiful oak trees off in the distance surrounding our little ballpark, three-fourths of a mile north of the Raccoon River. When the fall came and the leaves changed, it was a beautiful sight to behold.

Our field of dreams had everything. We installed benches and put in seats behind the chicken wire, which was about twelve feet high. We installed two outhouses, one for the ladies and one for the gentlemen. We charged 25 cents a game; doubleheaders were 35 cents. My father and I dragged the field by hand to keep it in shape. We built up the pitching mound, and any groundskeeper can tell you that building up a mound is one of the most important—and toughest—jobs in grounds keeping. We brought in the clay and tapped it down, sometimes using a pickup truck or a team of horses to do this. We even had our own soda pop stand!

In those days every small town had a baseball team. My dad was the manager of the Oak View team that played in our field of dreams, and he had most all of the young adults in the area playing on it. I was the only young kid there at the time (I was twelve years old), so I also played American Legion Ball. My dad booked the games for an entire season with teams from all over Iowa, and we also played around central Iowa. All of the young men played baseball on Sundays, and news of our field spread. We had a telephone party line with seventeen people, and word of mouth made our field a household name.

It was from the pitcher's mound in our field of dreams where my father pitched to me so often after school that I was prepared to advance to the major leagues. I could pitch at odd moments when other kids could not, so I practiced in a fifteen-minute block of time here and there, and all of a sudden I had an incredibly strong arm for my age. This made it possible for me to be known as a young phenom throughout Iowa.

As for the Sunday ritual of playing baseball and going to games, it was the norm back then. Nowadays, if you asked your girlfriend to come watch you play baseball on a Sunday afternoon, you'd lose a girlfriend. She'd probably go off with someone else who didn't care about baseball and would chauffeur her around in a new convertible. How times have changed.

If a father approached me to ask why he should invest all of the time necessary to building a field of dreams, I'd tell him that there is no greater reward in the world than enhancing your relationship with your child, and building a field of dreams will bring a father and child closer together. It will be invaluable to the child's educational process and invaluable to the father's relationship with his son or daughter. It will show the child that the father has the utmost confidence in him or her and thus will help the child mature. This was exactly how I felt when my dad and I worked side by side building the ball field on our farm. I knew my dad had confidence in me and that this was his way of displaying it.

Building a field of dreams gives a child something to be proud of, and something to keep in his or her heart forever. I recommend that every father who has the capability to do this for his child do it. The rewards will last a lifetime. I found something I loved to do, and consequently I never had to WORK a day in my life.

Thomas A. Edison said, "Decide what you like to do in life. Start young. Never work another day." Do what you like to do and become proficient at it and if you're lucky, it'll never feel as though you're working.

My Mom Was Always There for Me

My mother was not only a college graduate who taught school, she was a registered nurse as well. She worked in both fields until I came along in 1918. She continued to teach for awhile, but not for very long after because she wanted to be around when I came home from school.

My mother was always there when I came home. In all of the years until I left high school, I don't think my mother missed greeting me five times. I usually returned home around 4:15 or 4:30 from Van Meter, which was about three and a half miles from our farm. Mom was always there to meet me. It meant the world to me.

To me, a mother meeting her child when he or she comes home from school is paramount. If you're going to have children, you should stay home with them. It gives children a sense of security to know someone is waiting for them, and it prevents them from doing things after school that are bad for their moral values or their character.

My mother gave me something, as did my father, that was better than money or the keys to the car: quality time!

Backyard Games I Played with My Dad

My dad and I were always playing catch on our farm. We had not only our own field of dreams, but a barn built in 1886. (That barn, Feller Farmstead, is now in the National Register, along with the house I built for my parents in 1940.) My dad and I played many hours of catch, even in the backyard between the outhouse and the house, and it gave me the encouragement I needed to believe in my abilities. I was always throwing, so that's probably why my arm was so strong.

The barn was more than a barn. It was made of native lumber and built with pegs, no nails. We played ball on the second floor, keeping the livestock below and hay up above for insulation. We'd open the doors a bit to get enough light to see the ball. Later on we installed a windmill generator and strung lights all around so that we could see, and we had a gasoline engine generator as well—all before rural electrification came to our area!

Dad also would hit ground balls to me in the hog lot and pitch batting practice to me. We'd sew up the balls with harness thread, running them through beeswax to make them last longer.

My dad and I also had basketball hoops outside and in the barn. The memories surrounding the cold nights in Iowa playing underneath those hoops are as vivid today as they were some seventy years ago. I know that basketball did much for my physique and inner confidence.

All of these backyard games represented the time my dad spent with me and the love and support he gave me to pursue my career in professional baseball.

The Importance of Manual Labor

The ballplayers of my era had more stamina than the players do today, particularly the pitchers, because they often came from rural areas where they had to do lots of manual labor. Pitchers could go longer in a game. I myself pitched thirty-six complete games in 1936, the most complete games since 1916 (which was four years before the live ball was introduced). You must learn how to pace yourself.

I often get questions from parents about how to maximize their children's physical potential during the developmental stages. Unfortunately, the kids aren't going to like what I'm about to say, but it is in their best interest. The best type of physical workout plan children can have early in life is helping their parents with household chores. I say this because those chores—taking out the garbage, cleaning windows, cleaning the house—allow kids to lift weights without injury because the exercise is natural. Here was my workout routine as a child:

Milking the cows, picking the corn, and throwing bales of straw and hay around. Those bales of hay really helped strengthen my arms because long before I was a teenager, I was lifting sizable weights at different angles, as opposed to the gym where you do stylized exercises. Those hay bales were a great workout because I had to lift them sideways and toss them using the muscles in my wrists, hands, forearms, and back. This was the epitome of a complete workout, and since it was a big help to my parents, I was doing two things at once: weight training and helping out. If you're in the city and don't have the opportunity for this kind of labor, then use the weight rooms.

Feeding the hogs, pumping water, and cleaning the barns. I'd pump the water into the tank for the horses and the other livestock. I'd clean out the barn on Saturdays and take the manure out and put it in a pile. I was working all the time. My arms and legs were strong from this work. When people talk about a full-functioning farm, ours is what they're talking about in every sense of the word. We did our own slaughtering on the premises. We even made our own soap! We did everything on our farm. I worked with my dad and he and my mother never had to tell me what to do. I knew what had to be done, and anything I could do to help my parents I did without asking any questions.

Manual labor strengthened my young arms, which is exactly what a pitcher needs to be successful in the major leagues. This type of natural exercise was the best in the world, and the fact that my arm became strong was just a side benefit. The main reward was that I knew I was helping my parents out and that meant the most to me.

Why First Steps Are Important

Parents should listen to their kids and not just give them money. Some parents are always trying to entertain their children by having them watch television or play on the Internet. A child's first steps are important, and an athlete's first steps are important. No should mean no, not maybe. Kids should be taught consequences from an early age so that they are prepared for life, whether it be a life in athletics, science, music, law, or medicine. Kids will test the limits of authority, and a parent should be strong and should not collapse under pressure. It is not the coach's job to train young athletes to have character. That should have been done by the parents long before the coach enters the scene. Don't get education mixed up with common sense or with intelligence.

Common sense and responsibility in baseball—or in life for that matter—are not only important to survive in the game, but are important for your life after sports. No matter how great an athlete is, there must be a life after sports because you can only play so long. Baseball is a game that accurately teaches consequences. Sports, in general, teach children consequences and responsibility. As most athletes won't make the majors, the whole idea of involving a child in sports is to allow him or her to develop, have fun, and learn something of moral value. A child's first steps are important because many times a not-so-perfect child will stay that way unless he or she is taught discipline, and sports are an excellent avenue to teach children discipline and responsibility. Even if the goal of a child and his or her parents is to become a professional star athlete, the first steps are important because they precede everything. The first steps are the building blocks of character.

This country has been built on common sense and intelligence. We didn't become the greatest country on Earth by accident. Our forefathers were very intelligent and had great foresight in creating the Constitution and Bill of Rights. The Constitution allows for freedom of speech, but everyone should be taught that with freedom of speech comes consequences. You can't expect to insult somebody and then be surprised that they don't like you anymore. It is the parent's job to deliver, in the case of sports, a coachable young person to a coach or manager, so that the sports education can commence, rather than expecting the coach to be both sports instructor and spiritual instructor. The spiritual instruction and education of a child should be accomplished well before high school by the parents. The first thing I tell young pitchers or young players about talking to the media and to fans is to think before they open their mouths. Think about the impact of what they're saying!

What Babe Ruth Meant to Me

I first saw Babe Ruth play an exhibition game in Des Moines, Iowa, when I was a young lad in 1929. The Bustin' Babes and the Larapin Lou's were touring the Midwest. Babe and Lou Gehrig put on a hitting exhibition before the game, and Babe pitched one inning. I got my first autographed ball from him in Des Moines. I had to earn that autograph because first I had to hunt and catch gophers. My dad drove me to the county treasurer's office with the fifty gophers' feet and I received $5.00. (The county was collecting gopher's feet because the gophers were destroying the alfalfa and clover crops. I received a bounty of ten cents a pair.) I went down to the ballpark and bought the ball. That baseball, which has both Babe Ruth's and Lou Gehrig's signatures on it, is in my museum in Van Meter. Julia Ruth Stevens is a good friend of my wife, Anne, and she wrote a wonderful book on her life with her dad.

I got the chance to go to dinner with Babe Ruth as a young player in New York. Tom Meeny, the Yankees public relations director, arranged that meeting. Babe Ruth even leaned on my bat that fateful day of June 13, 1948, when the Yankees honored him on Babe Ruth Day. He used my bat as a cane to stand and prop himself up, and that's the one in the famous picture of Ruth leaning on a bat addressing the sold-out Yankee Stadium crowd. That bat was Bob Feller's bat, and I pitched the game that day at Yankee Stadium. Babe Ruth passed away two months later.

Speaking of pitching, Ruth was a terrific pitcher and if he had continued to pitch would have been a Hall of Fame pitcher. Ruth won eighteen games as a pitcher in 1915, twenty-three games in 1916, and twenty-four games in 1917. He won thirteen games in 1918 as a pitcher/outfielder, splitting his time between the two positions. As a hitter, Babe Ruth was the greatest. He ranks first all-time in slugging percentage, walks, and home runs per at bat. He ranks second all-time in home runs, RBIs, on-base percentage, and runs scored. He is in the top ten players in history in lifetime batting average, with a .342 career batting average, and he is in the top five of all time in total bases. He was clearly the most dominant player of his era or any other.

This is why Babe Ruth, to me, is the greatest player ever. He could pitch, play the outfield, hit for average, and hit for power. He ran the bases well, never threw to the wrong base, and had the best charisma of anybody. The Roaring Twenties brought prosperity to millions of Americans, and Babe Ruth represented the jovial nature of the era. Baseball used him to capitalize on these good times.

Signing My Pro Contract at Sixteen

When I signed my first baseball contract at the age of sixteen, between my sophomore and junior years of high school, I never had the intention of being anything other than a major league baseball player. This was probably very cocky for a kid who had been playing since age nine. When I was fifteen years old, I used to go out and pitch for $100 and a tank of gas from in-state baseball promoters and team managers. My father signed the contract with me, as my guardian. I received a check for $1.00 to make it legal. In fact, I still have that canceled check in my museum in Van Meter, Iowa. I also received a ball autographed by all the Cleveland Indians. I didn't care about how much money I was getting or the amount of the signing bonus. I just wanted the opportunity to play, even at the lowest level in Class D in Fargo, North Dakota, the Indians' farm club.

Cy Slapnicka was the scout who signed me and, coincidentally, he became general manager of the Cleveland Indians right after he signed me. He was one of the best scouts of all time. He signed some of the best players: Herb Score, Lou Boudreau, Mel Harder, and Hal Trosky.

Cy had been tipped off about me by a couple of umpires, John McMahon in particular, who were umpiring American Legion Ball. These scouts were called bird dogs because they received their pay according to what prospects they could obtain for the particular region of the country to which they were assigned. If the player was successful, the scout would receive his pay. If the player wasn't successful, the scout didn't get paid. Needless to say, the scout's reputation was built upon the actual success of his players, not the mere hype surrounding them.

My pilgrimage to the pros was not without consequence, as I became ineligible to play any high school sport because of my professional athletic status. I could not play basketball my senior year of high school because of my contract with the Cleveland Indians. The rule has since changed; if you play professional baseball, you can play another sport in high school. You're only considered a professional in the sport you're paid to play.

I pitched the 1936 Iowa State high school tournament and immediately afterward went to Cleveland so that the Indians officials could check me out. My arm was tired and the Indians wanted to see if it was still going to be in good condition. My arm proved to be fine, a benefit of being young and strong from all that farm labor. I pitched the fourth, fifth, and sixth innings of an exhibition game against the St. Louis Cardinals and struck out eight of the nine hitters I faced. Instead of going to Fargo, as originally planned, I went directly to Philadelphia and joined the major league Cleveland Indians, who were playing the Phillies. My job (called "mop-up") was to enter the game when it was already out of hand and save the other pitchers' arms. I got my first chance to start in a game in late August and finished the 1936 season having won five and lost three. My outings greatly impressed the Indians organization, and my job as their starter seemed just around the corner.

My first strikeout was Buddy Lewis, the Washington Senators' third baseman. The game was played in Washington, D.C., at Griffith Stadium. I had met Connie Mack, the owner and manager of the Philadelphia Athletics, two days before in Shibe Park, Philadelphia. He holds the record for consecutive years as a manager— more than fifty. Meeting him was important to me because he was an icon in baseball, scholar of the game, and well-respected gentleman.

No One's Immortal

I feel blessed to have been born to parents as great as mine. But no one's immortal—you have to realize that and do the best you can for people while they're here.

My father developed brain cancer in 1936. I was in the navy during World War II, but I felt that as long as I made sure my dad was receiving the best medical help possible, I was doing all I could for him. He died in 1943 while I was aboard ship. I returned home for his funeral.

My mother died of lung cancer at age 60, even though she never smoked. She knew what ailed her—after all, she was a registered nurse. She found out about her condition in September 1954 and could not attend the World Series in Cleveland that month. After the World Series, I took her to Mayo Clinic in Rochester, Minnesota, and they told me the doctor in Des Moines had diagnosed her cancer correctly. She died later that year.

Gates Mills, Ohio

Gates Mills has been my home since the summer of 1948, and now it represents the place where my wife, Anne, and I live. My son, Steve, designed the house for us. We make our home out in the woods, along with our black cat, Felix. Felix is our little pal; he follows me everywhere I go when I'm outside, and he follows Anne around when she's inside. We have a couple of barns, an ample amount of trees, a gazebo, a deck, and a patio. We also have our own well water and our own power with a full generator in case of an emergency. Living in Gates Mills allows me to stay at home and stay in touch with the Indians ball club in Cleveland, twenty-two miles away. This is important because I am still employed by the Cleveland Indians.

My Special Hobby

I started collecting Caterpillar tractors about fifteen years ago. I worked it out with my cousin in Iowa and I have five of them in Cleveland now. They are small to medium-sized tractors to be restored, repainted, and shown at shows in the Midwest. The reason I collect Caterpillar can be traced back to my childhood. I used to drive a tractor on my dad's farm in Iowa, and we had one of the first Caterpillar tractors and combines this side (east) of the Missouri River. Everybody said the crops wouldn't ripen properly, but they did. We did custom combing for our neighbors for $2.00 an acre and 10 cents a bushel.

I use the tractors at my home in Gates Mills, Ohio, to drag the logs. I also have a new Massen Ferguson tractor with all the attachments, which excites me.

Family Values

Most ballplayers eventually get married and have children. Ballplayers are home with their families more than most businessmen because they have what is called an off-season. There isn't any off-season in the corporate world. During the regular season, when the ball club is home, they're home. Athletes many times have their kids with them at the ballpark. Kids today can even follow their dads via satellite when the team is on the road.

Family values are important because when things are not going well, you can always count on your kids to run to you and support you—win or lose. Family values impact the game of baseball greatly. I hope the ballplayers heed my words and think about the personal decisions they make in their lives, as it will impact their playing careers and their lives after baseball.

PART II

My Baseball Days:
The Game, the People,
the Glory

The Day I Struck Out Eighteen Batters

I struck out eighteen batters in Cleveland on October 1, 1938, the last day of the season. It was the first game of a doubleheader against the Detroit Tigers, and my catcher was Frank Pytlak. The last batter was Chet Laabs, whom I struck out five times that day. He swung fourteen times, took the last pitch for a called third strike, and argued with the umpire over the call. I had a great curveball that day (not at all uncommon for me, as I had been throwing curves since I was eight years old), and I procured many strikeouts with it. I was also fortunate enough to get many called third strikes.

This day was a great accomplishment on my baseball resume. In 1936, at age seventeen, I had broken the American League record with seventeen strikeouts in a single game, which tied Dizzy Dean's National League record. The Tigers had six hits that day in October, and the game meant absolutely nothing to the team's standing. The only thing it did mean was that I was now the strikeout king for a single game.

The Motorcycle Test

The motorcycle test was the luckiest thing that ever happened in my life. It was conducted in 1940, in Chicago. Lou Fonseca was running the Major League Baseball Film Division in the Chicago office of the commissioner of baseball. Judge Kennesaw Mountain Landis was commissioner at that time, and his office was at 333 North Michigan Avenue. Lou himself had been a batting champion when he led the American League in 1929. He came to see me when we played the White Sox at Comiskey Park and told me that he was going to have me throw against a speeding motorcycle the following day.

We held the test in Lincoln Park, right near Lake Michigan on the North Side. The city police department even blocked off the street for this experiment. I went in my street clothes, wearing a dress shirt and tie. I had no idea about the particulars of the test when Lou picked me up at the Del Prado Hotel at 53rd and Hyde Park Avenue that day. He brought along the gloves and balls and gave me some details about how they intended to time my pitch using the motorcycle.

When we got to Lincoln Park, Lou showed me the targets. The bull's-eye was about the size of a cantaloupe. I warmed up and then wanted to take my full windup, but Lou told me to stand as if a man were on base, so I could watch the motorcycle take off.

I didn't listen to him and took a full windup because I thought it would help me throw much harder. I was very lucky to hit the target. The motorcycle got a head start on me, although I hadn't planned on that. The luckiest part of the whole thing was that the ball went right through the middle of the bull's-eye. I never thought I could do it, at least not the way that Lou Fonseca had asked me to. I thought I'd be lucky to hit the target at all. There was no trickery or Hollywood-type shots. It was just like you see it on the videotape, on the first try, with two very good cameramen doing their job perfectly. I'm glad the ball hit the target that afternoon, or I might still be out there throwing.

The speed of the ball was clocked at 104 mph. We calculated it as follows: I gained 13 feet on the motorcycle at 60 feet, 6 inches, and the motorcycle was traveling at 86 mph ($86 \div 60.5 = 1.42$; $13 + 60.5 = 73.5 \times 1.42 = 104$).

Later, I threw to the full electric zone devices at the Aberdeen Ordinance Plant in Washington, D.C., and was clocked at 107.9 mph, the fastest pitch ever tested with a speed-measuring device.

If someone were to ask me who the fastest pitcher in the history of the game was, I'd say Walter Johnson, but he never was clocked. He did not, however, have a curveball. I had the fastball, curveball, slider, and change-up.

What fills me with great pride to this day is that major league baseball is still showing the footage of me throwing the ball through the bull's-eye and the motorcycle crashing through the target during rain delays and at opening-day ceremonies. I myself sometimes take that footage with me when I make a speech. I'll start off with the motorcycle test, and then I'll show the famous and hilarious Abbott and Costello skit of "Who's on First?" The audience usually responds favorably, and then I'll give my talk and take questions. The motorcycle test, to me, is not only a documentation of how fast a pitcher I was in my youth, but it is a testament to the times before the radar gun and all of the statistics. When I hit that bull's-eye and my fastball was officially "clocked," it was a scientific happening in the game of baseball.

Baseball now uses the wonders of science and technology—fast-developing film, laptop computers, and radar guns—to clock the speed of a pitcher's ball. Although I had no idea of the future when I stood on that blocked-off street, I did know that something special was happening. I'm glad to have helped satisfy some of the curiosity about pitchers and the speed with which they throw the ball.

Three No-Hitters

No-hitters have all of the drama of a Broadway play: suspense, despair (if you lose), and elation when it's all over. I attribute my three no-hitters to three basic ingredients: hard work, determination, and great defense!

My first no-hitter came on opening day at Chicago's Comiskey Park in 1940. On a cold, Norway-gray day, with the temperature of Lake Michigan at 35°F and the wind blowing off the lake, I had my date with destiny. My dad, mother, and sister were in the stands to watch me. I had the bases loaded in the second inning and struck out the last hitter to retire the side. My roommate, Jeff Heath, had a single. My catcher, Rollie Helmsley, hit a triple up the alley in right center field in the fourth inning and brought in Jeff Heath. In the ninth inning with two out, Luke Appling came up for the Sox and fouled off two balls on about eight or ten pitches. I decided to walk him intentionally and threw two pitches outside, without telling Rollie. The last hitter was Taft Wright, who had always been a tough hitter for me. The tying run was on first base and Taft hit a smash between first base and second base. Ray Mack, the Indians' second baseman, dove for the ball, fell on his stomach, leaped up, grabbed the ball bare-handed, and whipped around to his left to fire it to Hal Trosky at first. The throw beat Taft Wright by a step, and the game was over. We won 1–0. Great defense by my teammate, Ray Mack, helped preserve my first no-hitter and the only opening-day no-hitter to date in major-league history.

My second no-hitter came on April 30, 1946, against the New York Yankees at Yankee Stadium after I rejoined the Cleveland Indians from my tour of duty in the navy. We won that game 1–0 as well. Frankie Hayes hit a home run off Bill Bevens about thirty rows deep into the left-center field bleachers. The bottom of the ninth inning saw Snuffy Stirnweiss get on base by way of an infielder's error on a ground ball with no one out. Tommy Henrich got Snuffy over to second base with a sacrifice bunt. Joe DiMaggio then grounded out to Lou Boudreau, and Stirnweiss went to third. My fastball and curveball were really on that day. Charlie Keller was the last hitter in the game. Charlie didn't like my curveball too much, and I threw him a high fastball out of the strike zone. He swung at it and missed. I then threw him a big, overhand curveball. He choked his bat and hit a real easy ground ball to second baseman Ray Mack, who in turn threw to Les Fleming at first base to end the game. We only got four hits ourselves in that game, so it was a real pitching duel. This was my best no-hitter.

As for my third no-hitter, that came five years later on July 1, 1951, against the Detroit Tigers at Cleveland's Municipal Stadium. On my second-to-last pitch in the ninth inning, Vic Wertz hit a ball four feet foul into the upper deck. He then took a called third strike for the final out, and we won the game by a score of 2–1. What I remember most about this game is that in one inning we made two errors and I still managed to throw a no-hitter. I tried to pick off a hitter who had reached first base on an error, but I threw the ball into center field. Fortunately for me, I still got the victory.

All-Star Game Memories

I was privileged to be on many an All-Star team. My first was the 1938 team. Although it was an honor and a privilege to be on the team, I did not appear in the game. That was the year that Johnny Vander Meer pitched back-to-back no-hitters. The National League won the game in Cincinnati, and Johnny and I became friends; he ended up finishing his career in Cleveland as my teammate. The game gave me the opportunity to observe Johnny, and I noticed that he had a great, live fastball.

The year 1939 saw me make my second pilgrimage to the Summer Classic, as the All-Star game has been dubbed by baseball media and fans. That year, Yankees manager Joe McCarthy was the manager of the American League team. He called me into the game in the sixth inning to relieve Tommy Bridges with the bases loaded and Arky Vaughan at the plate with one out.

I had seen Arky Vaughan play for Wichita in the Western League. I knew him to be a great fastball hitter. Bill Dickey visited the pitcher's mound and conferred with me concerning how to pitch to Vaughan. We decided to throw him a big, overhand fastball because we felt that with all of the white shirts in the Yankee Stadium bleachers, the pitch might be disguised a bit and give Vaughan some trouble as to location and speed. I threw that ball thinking he might not be able to get around on it, but he did. He hit a hard ground ball to Joe Gordon at second base. Gordon threw to Joe Cronin at shortstop, who in turn covered the second base bag, and then threw the ball to Hank Greenberg at first base to end the inning. I pitched the seventh, eighth, and ninth innings, striking out the last two hitters, Johnny Mize and Stan Hack. The American League won the game 3–1. I was not the winning pitcher, but that was my best All-Star appearance. If there had been such a thing as a save back then, I would have gotten credit for one.

My next All-Star team was in 1941. I started the game and pitched to the first nine hitters. The first hitter singled, but I picked him off at first base. This was the famous All-Star game in Detroit where Ted Williams hit the home run in the bottom of the ninth to win it. Joe DiMaggio had reached first base on what should have been the last out of the game, but Cecil Travis went into second base with his spikes high and hit Billy Herman, the National League second baseman. Billy made a wide throw to first base, pulling the first baseman off the base, and allowing DiMaggio to beat the throw. Ted Williams then hit Claude Passeau's pitch four feet fair on the top of the facade at Tiger Stadium to win the ballgame. Ted had timed it perfectly, and we won the game 7–5. Enos Slaughter retrieved that ball after it bounced back onto the field and gave it to Ted several years later.

I had served my country in the navy during World War II, losing four years of my playing career, but I had been lucky enough to return home and I was thankful to God. I was on the Service Team in 1942, when we played the American League All-Stars in Cleveland. The American League won the game 3–1. All the money we took in went to army-navy relief and to the widows and families of the men who had died during the attack on Pearl Harbor.

I went back to the All-Stars in 1946. I pitched the first three innings of the game, which was held at Fenway Park that year, and we won the game 12–0. Ted Williams hit two home runs, one off Rick Sewell's blooper pitch. That "blooper-pitch homer" went about thirty rows deep into the center-field bleachers.

I did not go to the 1947 All-Star game in Chicago, even though I had been selected. I was injured and could not play. I had hurt my back after striking out ten of the first twelve batters in Philadelphia prior to the All-Star game and had to leave the mound. I called Joe Cronin, who was managing the American League team, and told him I couldn't go. Joe asked me to suggest someone who could relieve me. I suggested Spec Shea, a young pitcher for the New York Yankees. Spec not only was selected to play for me, but he ended up being the winning pitcher that year. I never did pitch in Wrigley Field during my career.

In 1948 I was again chosen for the All-Star team, but I was having a terrible year and I refused to go, so someone else went in my place. I had no reason to be on the

All-Star team, except for old time's sake, and I knew I didn't deserve the honor.

The Windy City showcased the 1950 Summer Classic. The Chicago White Sox played host to quite a few dramatic baseball events. There was the Babe Ruth so-called shot back in the 1930s at Wrigley Field, and then there was the 1950 All-Star game where the American League lost in fourteen innings. I pitched in the eighth and ninth innings and managed to retire the men I faced. Little did I know this would be my last All-Star appearance and the end of my dominance in the Summer Classics.

1954's 111 Wins: The Best Ever?

In 1954 the Cleveland Indians won 111 games, which was the highest winning percentage since the Chicago Cubs won 116 in 1906. We had a better percentage than the 1998 World Champion New York Yankees when they won 114 games in a 162-game schedule, even though the Yankees went on to win the World Series in four straight games. They had a very well-balanced ball club and so did we, but our team was beaten in four straight by the red-hot New York Giants. Sal Maglie, Willie Mays, and Monte Irvin all made us look bad. Rochester native Johnny Antonelli, whose pitches were unhittable, made us look especially bad because he kept our bats as silent as lambs. Al Smith, our first batter, hit a home run in the

Polo Grounds, and that was the biggest noise we made the entire series.

The Best Catchers

Bill Dickey was the best all-around catcher to whom I've ever pitched. People sometimes give me a puzzled look because I played for the Indians and Bill played for the New York Yankees. What about the All-Star games?

I immediately think back to the 1939 All-Star game at Yankee Stadium when Joe McCarthy was managing the American League team. We won the game 3–1 and beat the National League. I entered the game and relieved Tommy Bridges of the Tigers in the sixth inning. There was one out and Arky Vaughan was at bat with the bases loaded. My first pitch was a fastball. Arky hit a two-hopper to second base to Joe Gordon, who threw to Joe Cronin at shortstop, who in turn threw to first base to complete the inning-ending double play. I pitched the seventh, eighth, and ninth innings for the American League to preserve the win.

I also pitched to Bill Dickey in the 1941 All-Star game in Detroit when Ted Williams hit a home run with two outs in the ninth inning to win the ballgame 7–5. I saw Bill catch a lot against the Indians and I always made sure to observe the way he called a game and the manner in which he played baseball. Jim Hegan might be better defensively and Frankie Hayes was a little better at calling pitches. Rollie Helmsley was an excellent catcher and was faster on the base paths than Bill Dickey, but Bill gets the nod as the best in my book, with Rollie Helmsley a close second place.

Bill Dickey could hit for average, a lifetime .313 hitter. He had a great arm to throw runners out at second base who were trying to steal. He was tall. He had excellent range because of his height. He had excellent judgment behind the plate and was a real Yankee all the way. I say that because he exhibited the class and dignity that the Yankees are always bragging about. In my book he is the best catcher I've ever pitched to because he had the total package. I'd also like to mention that while some great baseball players have made cameo appearances in some major movies, Bill gave an excellent performance in *The Pride of the Yankees*, alongside the great Gary Cooper and Theresa Wright. This movie was not only good for baseball, it was a fine motion picture, and I've seen it many times. I still regard the movie as one of the most sentimental tearjerkers of all time.

The Best Double-Play Tandems

Usually the teams with the best double-play combinations have the worst pitching. In other words, they turn the most double plays because there are always men on base! The Chicago Cubs had a great double-play tandem. Tinker to Evers to Chance is a famous tandem, but I like our

Cleveland tandem of Lou Boudreau at shortstop and Joe Gordon or Ray Mack at second base. Ray had been a football player and, for the runners, it was like sliding into a concrete wall. Lou and Ray could turn the double play as well as any tandem.

The Yankees had Bobby Richardson at second base who could turn a good double play, as could Bill Mazeroski of the Pittsburgh Pirates. The Yankees' Phil Rizzuto could turn the double play well in his day. Double-play combinations were especially important to our club because Mel Harder and Bob Lemon were sinker ball pitchers, which is why Boudreau, Mack, and Gordon were extremely valuable. Sinker ball pitchers need a good double-play tandem behind them because they usually have many ground balls hit to the infield. Screwball pitchers and control pitchers also need a good double-play tandem behind them.

As a fan, you can play the role of scout and assess what I've said. Just observe the teams with great double-play tandems—those are the teams that are constantly allowing the opposition to put the ball in play. Again, the worst pitching staffs have the most double-play combinations because they always have men on base.

The Toughest Outs

The hitters who don't swing hard are the toughest to get out. This has always been my motto when it comes to hitters. The most dangerous are those who just meet the ball. They can turn a pitcher's win into a loss at light speed.

Tommy Henrich, Stan Spence, Nellie Fox, Johnny Pesky, and Bobby Doerr were all tough outs because they just met the ball and went with the pitch. Joe DiMaggio was another tough out and got ten or eleven home runs off me. Ted Williams never hit a home run off me before World War II, but he got eleven home runs off me after the war. Bobby Doerr got ten off of me, most of which I gave up in Fenway Park.

My approach to these players was as follows. Usually the slider was the best pitch to the left-handed hitters. A high, tight fastball was best to right-handed hitters, if you could throw it hard enough to get it by them.

I would often speak with other pitchers around the league as to how to pitch to certain hitters. We used to do it all the time, back when I played. I would call up Ted Lyons or Allie Reynolds, and I'd talk with Lefty Grove as well. I'd call them on the road and get their advice, but I'd only talk to pitchers who had the same pitching style as I had.

Pitchers Who Could Hit Well

Bob Lemon was one of the best hitting pitchers, as he first came up to the big leagues as an infielder/outfielder. However, his pitching stints in Hawaii during World War

II kept his pitching arm in shape and helped him get noticed as a pitcher. Red Ruffing was a very good hitter as well. Cy Young and Walter Johnson were very fine hitting pitchers, although they were best known for their astonishing win totals. Wes Ferrell had the most home runs of any pitcher, making him one of the all-time best hitting pitchers. Wes was an excellent pitcher and is in the Hall of Fame. Lemon was close to Ferrell in lifetime home runs for a pitcher, but Lemon had several of his home runs as an infielder/outfielder.

There's a story that surrounds one of the worst hitting pitchers, Hall of Famer Lefty Gomez. Lefty once bet Babe Ruth $100 that he could get five hits in a single season. On opening day, he got four hits in the game he pitched, and still went on to lose the bet! He never got another hit that entire season.

My Cleveland Teammates: Bob Lemon, Early Wynn, and Al Rosen

Bob Lemon started out as an infielder, but since we had Kenny Keltner at third base, they placed him in center field in 1946. Bob had pitched a lot in the navy during World War II. Bob couldn't hit enough to be a center fielder so Lou Boudreau, our manager, placed Bob on the mound. Nineteen forty-six saw the pitching debut of Bob

Lemon, and he became a phenomenal pitcher. A Hall of Famer, Bob literally went from saving my ballgame on opening day in 1946 by throwing to and doubling a man off second base after a daring catch in center field to taking the pitcher's mound and becoming a tremendous pitcher. Bob had a good curve, a good slider, and a vicious sinker pitch. He wasn't overly fast, but he always stayed ahead of the hitters and he didn't walk many batters, which is the key to success in the majors. When Bob passed away in 2000, it saddened me deeply.

Early Wynn was another friend of mine on the Indians who won more than 300 games, his 300th with the Indians. Early had a good fastball, a really good change-up, and a really good slider. He had good control and, like Bob, did not walk many hitters. They were the heart and soul of the Cleveland pitching staff in the early 1950s. If Lemon and Wynn had not lost time in military service, their records would have been considerably better.

Al Rosen took over for Kenny Keltner in 1950 and became the regular Cleveland Indians third baseman. Al turned out to be an excellent third baseman and a great hitter. He had an outstanding All-Star game in Cleveland in 1954, when he hit two home runs and helped the American League defeat the National League by a score of 11–9. He was a good clutch hitter, a good team player, and great in the clubhouse. He had a fine wife, Terri, and a nice family. He was a close friend of Larry Doby. Al was a great team leader, a great team captain, and a good businessman. He was also a terrific general manager, and a good president of the New York Yankees.

Al has always taken good care of his health, from his playing days until the present, and he never abused his body. I'm proud to say that he was my teammate in 1954, and although we lost the series to the Giants, Al was a great team leader in the clubhouse. The Giants just stopped us cold with their great pitching.

Yogi Berra

Yogi was a great hitter, a great catcher, and brutal in the outfield! A three-time MVP award winner, Yogi is a classic in and out of baseball. He is known to the world as both a baseball player and a philosopher. His wisdom will last forever. I think some of those oddball sayings, however, were made up by Joe Garagiola's joke writers. My favorite Yogi-ism is, "When you're lost and come to a fork in the road, take it."

The Yankees had a Hall of Fame catcher, yet they tried to make an outfielder out of him, and that was a mistake. Catching was his forte and he was one of the greatest of all time. In addition to being superb behind the plate, Yogi shone as a hitter.

Yogi would swing at just about anything! He had no weak spots. The best way to get him out was to throw the ball right down the middle, belt-high. Your chances of getting him out were as good as if you threw the ball right over his head or two inches off his shoelaces. He had great wrists and could quickly turn on the ball and pull it for a home run. He could hit home runs in any ballpark. He had a tremendous amount of upper body strength, and that's why he had such a productive career as a catcher.

On a personal note, Carmen and Yogi Berra are dear friends of mine. Anne and I always enjoy seeing them at Cooperstown induction weekend. He is a major Hall of Famer in my book, and his persona on and off the field gave the Yankees of the 1950s and 1960s much character and class.

The Boones: Three Generations in Baseball

It is rare that you find a father-son team, much less a grandfather-father-son team, in baseball or any other professional sport. Ray Boone, Bob Boone, and Brett and Aaron Boone are the first three-generation sports family.

Ray Boone is someone I know quite well from our days playing together on the Cleveland Indians. Ray was a very good low-ball hitter. He had quite a bit of power. He was not much of a shortstop, but became an excellent third baseman. He was no Kenny Keltner, but he was very good. He could go to his left and right and played the position well. At the plate, Boone was a dangerous hitter. He had power and could take you deep if you were not careful in how you pitched him. In 1955 he drove in 116 runs for the Detroit Tigers, and it was not too long after that another Boone entered the baseball scene.

Bob Boone, Ray Boone's son, was a terrific catcher who caught almost 2,000 games. He was a player representative and always possessed good leadership qualities. His sons, Brett and Aaron, now play for the San Diego Padres and Cincinnati Reds, respectively.

The whole Boone family are good friends of mine. They are a credit to baseball and to the United States of America. Ray's wife, Pat, is a great wife, mother, and grandmother.

Lou Boudreau

Lou Boudreau was afraid of nobody. A legitimate Hall of Famer, he was not only a great leader as a player and manager, but he was a stellar athlete in another sport—basketball.

Many people don't realize that Lou played basketball for the University of Illinois and was part of the "Whiz Kids" team at college. He had such great peripheral vision that I often remark that he was able to see behind him. He was a great passer and a great dribbler. However, he was slow afoot. Basketball was there for Lou, but he decided to make baseball his vocation and, for my sake, I'm glad he did.

Lou was terrific as a teammate in every respect. He knew how to give encouragement and how to relate to other players. As a baseball player, he could both hit well and field well, and was an especially excellent doubles hitter, three times leading the American League in doubles in a single season. Defensively, he could go to his right very well. He anticipated where the ball was going to be hit and that made him an exceptional shortstop. In fact, in my book he is the King of Shortstops. Lou Boudreau was better than any shortstop I ever saw!

A major Hall of Famer, Lou was able to finish his stellar playing career and then go on to manage and win as a manager. Lou was a better player-manager than a bench manager. I remember he went 4–4 in the sudden death playoff game with the Boston Red Sox in 1948. The Indians had finished the season tied with Boston, and Lou's 4–4 day made it possible for us to go the World Series. We didn't even have to travel to get to the series because the Boston Braves club was our National League opponent. We stayed in Boston after that sudden death playoff game, and then proceeded to finish the job and win the World Series. Lou showed the world that a player-manager can help his club both at the plate and from inside the dugout.

I'm glad to have been Lou's teammate. I'm even prouder to call him my friend.

Joe DiMaggio: The Yankee Clipper

Joe came up to the majors in 1936. Four years older than I was, he became a bona fide star right away, winning Rookie of the Year, even though a fellow by the name of Bo Bell had a great year in St. Louis.

Joe was the toughest right-handed hitter I ever faced. He could not hit a sinker and I, ironically, could not throw a sinker. Joe could not hit Mel Harder or Bob Lemon very well because they were sinker ball pitchers. Joe was an excellent fastball hitter, however, and hit me well. He had a spread batting stance and would pull the ball. However, his wide stance made it difficult for him to move. He was a sweep hitter and if you threw a ball close to him he was going to get a hit. But he often could not get out of the way of an inside pitch because of this wide batting stance.

I used to pitch him outside a lot because I didn't want to hit him and he just kept wearing me out. Finally I got enough nerve to pitch him inside, though. I then started to have success with Joe DiMaggio.

Joe was an excellent center fielder. He had an exceptionally accurate arm, as well as great intuition. He knew where to play the ball to get the best possible jump on it. However, his one foible was that he could not run the bases too well. He was a pretty decent base runner as far as intuition goes, but he could not steal bases. He could not get the same jump on a pitcher on the base paths as a runner that he could as a center fielder on balls hit to the outfield. When a ball was hit to the outfield, he could take off and arrive in plenty of time. When it came to getting a jump on the pitcher to steal a base, however, he just didn't shine. DiMaggio was a dramatic player, however, and his image of greatness is well deserved because of his hitting ability, his fielding ability, and his persona on and off the field. His marriage to Marilyn Monroe gave him much unnecessary publicity, which perhaps was unfortunate for Joe's sake.

If you were a National League fan you might say Willie Mays or Duke Snider was the best at center field. However, I didn't see much of them and, being an American League player, I'd have to give the nod to Joe DiMaggio as my top pick in center field for my era. I considered my friendship with Joe to be something special and was proud to play in his charity Joe DiMaggio Classic to benefit the Fort Lauderdale Children's Hospital. Baseball will miss Joe.

His lifetime stats deserve recognition. Here was a man who lost time to World War II and still compiled a lifetime batting average of .325 and a slugging percentage of .579. Joe was a two-time batting champion and, more important, a three-time American League Most Valuable Player. His 56-consecutive-game hitting streak still stands and will always be a great baseball feat.

The day that 56-game hitting streak came to an end I was in the Cleveland dugout. The game was played in Municipal Stadium in Cleveland, and Joe hit some very hard ground balls on short hops down the left field line. Lou Boudreau made a very good play that day on a ball that took a bad hop. Boudreau bare-handed it and threw to first for the putout. Joe, throughout the entire night of hard-hit ground balls, never showed any emotion. He didn't kick first base, or second base, or the dirt. He headed toward the dugout as if he'd hit the ball out of the ballpark. I'm sure, knowing Joe, that it was all built up inside him. Joe was a class act on and off the field.

Larry Doby: A Pioneer in the American League

Larry Doby was the first African American in the American League, debuting just weeks after Jackie Robinson debuted in the National League. I met Larry when he joined our club in Chicago, and Lou Boudreau, our player-manager, introduced him to all of us. He was befriended by myself, Lou Boudreau, Joe Gordon, and Bob Lemon.

Larry came up at second base and was quickly moved to center field. He became an outstanding center fielder and made many an All-Star team. Larry won a lot of ball games for the Indians with his power at the plate. He was a long-ball hitter, and I was glad to have him as a teammate. Larry still lives in New Jersey, and he is a credit to the game of baseball and to the Indians ball club.

Double X: Jimmie Foxx

Jimmie Foxx was a very powerful fellow. He was a right-handed hitter and a low-ball hitter, and could hit a ball a mile. He was a very good friend of mine.

Jimmie hit knuckleballs very well, and it was tough for the infielders and outfielders to catch the vicious line drives off his bat because the baseball, when hit, did not rotate at all. Some of those balls flew past the infielders or outfielders as if Hoyt Wilhelm had thrown the ball himself. Jimmie hit 58 home runs one year and he hit balls farther than anyone. He was a dangerous hitter and an excellent first baseman as well. He had a lifetime batting average of .325. He compiled an incredible .428 on-base percentage and a career .609 slugging percentage, finishing with 534 career home runs, 1,351 runs scored, and 1,922 RBIs.

Most of all, however, Jimmie Foxx was a likable guy. I don't think Jimmie had any enemies. He died fairly young, and his nickname "Double X" was because his last name had two x's in it. Jimmie had a son who played in

the same league I managed, the American Amateur Baseball Congress League in Lakewood, Ohio, for college
boys. He was a third baseman, a tall kid, taller than his
dad, but not as powerful or as muscular.

Charlie Gehringer: The Mechanical Man

Quiet Charlie Gehringer was known by his peers as The
Mechanical Man. He never said much and was always in
the right place at the right time. He was what we called a
guess hitter, and he guessed right a lot because his lifetime
average was .320 and he had seven seasons of 200 hits or
more in a single season. I saw Charlie play in the 1934
World Series, when the Detroit Tigers were beaten by the
St. Louis Cardinals in seven games. I remember Dizzy
Dean won the last game in Detroit 11–0. I personally
attended the three games played in St. Louis. I saw Dizzy
Dean win, and his brother Paul win, during those three
games, and saw Gehringer's prowess at the plate as well.

Charlie was highly thought of by everyone in baseball.
He was a gentleman and a great second baseman.

Henry "Hank" Benjamin Greenberg

Hank Greenberg hit 58 home runs in 1938, but the last
four games in Cleveland he didn't hit any, managing to hit

only a double. All the sportswriters were in attendance, thinking that this might be the year that Babe Ruth's record would fall, but Hank didn't make it. He finished his career in Pittsburgh in 1947. When they cut down the left field fence and installed a bull pen, that area became known as Greenberg Gardens because Hank would hit mammoth home runs that would land there. Later, that area became known as Kiner's Korner. Hank took Ralph Kiner under his wing and gave him the necessary tutelage to enable Ralph to rise to unheralded stardom of his own.

Hank had a lifetime batting average of .313, a lifetime on-base percentage of .412, a lifetime slugging percentage of .605, and 331 lifetime home runs. He led the American League four times in home runs and, in addition to being an MVP, drove in 100 or more RBIs in a season seven times in his career.

Hank became the general manager of the Indians, taking over for Bill Veeck, and Ralph finished his playing career with Cleveland as well. Hank's sons became friends with my sons, and they went to private school together. Hank's death saddened me. I always regarded him as a great person, which was even more important to me than his great ballplayer status.

Mel Harder

When Larry Dolan bought the Indians from my friend Richard Jacobs, I had the opportunity to speak with

Larry. We both immediately agreed—having deep roots in Cleveland—that Mel Harder belonged in the Baseball Hall of Fame in Cooperstown, New York. We thought for sure Mel would make it in 2000, but he didn't and it saddened me. Mel was not only a great pitcher, winning 223 games and having two 20-plus winning seasons, but he was an excellent pitching coach. He never made you throw the way he threw; he observed his pitchers and had them throw the way they threw when they were at their best on the mound.

Mel threw an excellent sinker ball when he was a player. In fact, he had tremendous success against one of baseball's greatest players, Joe DiMaggio, because of his sinker ball. Mel was signed by Cy Slapnicka, as was I, and we remain great friends to this day.

Richard Jacobs: A Good Friend

Richard Jacobs was the owner of the Cleveland Indians who saved baseball in that city. He isn't the owner any more, but his presence will be felt forever. He built one of the best fields in history. Richard was a hands-off owner; he didn't bother the manager or the general manager. He developed shopping malls across the United States. He is quiet and humble, a charitable man, and a tremendous asset to the Cleveland area. He was instrumental in building a statue of me, which was one of the nicest honors I ever received.

Under Mr. Jacobs, the Indians began a new era of tradition, pride, and excellence. The 1994 Indians were a solid team, and in 1995 they won the American League Eastern Division, took the pennant, and played a hard-fought World Series against Atlanta. In 1996 the team again won their division, and in 1997 they reached the World Series once more, only to lose to the Florida Marlins in a dramatic seven games in extra innings. Both 1998 and 1999 also saw the Indians become a winning ball club. (The Indians have since been sold to Larry Dolan.)

The success of the Indians is attributable to Richard Jacobs and his style of ownership. Players such as Jim Thome, Manny Ramirez, Omar Vizquel, Sandy Alomar Jr., Kenny Lofton, and Charles Nagy have been important Indian talents who were all signed during the Jacobs years.

Ralph Kiner: Kiner's Korner

Ralph will forever be known as a Hall of Fame baseball player, a broadcaster extraordinaire for the New York Mets, a great after-dinner speaker, and an all-around great human being, which is the most important quality anyone can have in my opinion.

Ralph was someone I always took on my barnstorming tours because he was such a great ballplayer. His average number of home runs per at bat is second only to Babe Ruth's. He averaged 1 home run per 14 at bats for an entire career. The number is still mind-boggling to me.

I played with Ralph in Mexico City and, with the 7,700-foot altitude, he could hit the balls out of sight. He hit balls 600 feet because of the thin air. I know one day he just kept hitting one 600-foot home run after the next. However, when we played in Tampico, just 40 feet above sea level, with the densest air around, he would hit home runs 200 feet less than in Mexico City. So his 600-foot homers in Mexico City were just 400-foot homers in Tampico. At first Ralph couldn't figure it out, and we used to rib him that he was losing his strength.

Ralph hit 369 lifetime home runs in only ten seasons before having to retire because of crippling back injuries. He won seven home run crowns in a row, from 1946 to 1952! Kiner's Korner was the bullpen area in Pittsburgh's Forbes Field into which Ralph would hit his home runs.

Ralph could turn on a ball just like his mentor and friend, Hank Greenberg. Ralph had exceptionally strong hands and forearms, and he could quickly get around on many pitches, turning them into home runs or extra base hits. The balls would leave the yard like homesick angels!

Today Ralph is still being recognized by millions of fans in New York on his show, "Kiner's Korner," and I can honestly say that Ralph achieved Hollywood success and stardom in an era when athletes were not seen on television. If you wanted to know what an athlete looked like and you couldn't come to the ballpark, you had to wait for a photo in the paper or a Movietone newsreel.

That tells you how well recognized Ralph Kiner was back in the 1940s and 1950s.

Mickey Mantle: The Commerce Comet

Mickey Mantle personified the small-town kid who made good. He and his dad played together like my dad and I did when I was young. Mickey Mantle had a great physique and was fast afoot. He had tremendous power and in my book he was a better left-handed hitter than right-handed hitter, even though right-hand was his natural side. He could hit a ball equally far from both sides of the plate. He liked the ball low in the strike zone, and if you were unlucky enough as a pitcher to give in to him, he could scoop up the low balls and lift them into the bleachers in right field at Yankee Stadium.

In the field he was speedy as well, and while his defense might not have been as good as Willie Mays', he was exceptionally fast on the base paths. He was the ultimate clutch hitter. When the game was on the line, Mickey always came through, and as a pitcher he was the last guy you'd want to see up at the plate in a key situation.

His osteomyelitis in his leg caused him to limp, but his career was stellar in spite of his physical ailments, which is a tribute to him as an athlete. He could still get to first base in about 3.3 seconds. If he hit a high hopper to an infielder, it was an automatic infield single. He could outrun all of those high hoppers. He helped define the Yankees, and taking over for Joe DiMaggio was no easy task either on or off the field.

Mantle had staggering lifetime numbers as well. He won the Triple Crown in 1956 and finished his career with a .298 lifetime batting average, 536 home runs, 2,415 hits, a .557 slugging percentage, and an on-base percentage of over .400.

I pitched to Mickey quite a bit and he did not hit the Cleveland pitchers quite as well as other pitchers in the league, but he hit the left-handed pitchers on the Cleveland club quite well from the right side of the plate. Was he better than Duke Snider or Willie Mays? To me, it's a matter of opinion. Was he better than DiMaggio? He didn't get as much publicity as DiMaggio. He didn't throw quite as well as Joe, but ran the bases much better. Could he cover as much ground as Joe? He certainly could.

Mickey's downfall lay in the fact that once baseball was over, he did not have any hobbies, and so he abused himself. He had too much extra time on his hands and that possibly led to his early death in 1996, which deeply saddened me.

Willie Mays: The Say Hey Kid

Every Giants fan went to see Willie Mays play in the Polo Grounds. I'm quite sure that each of those fans will tell you that he was the greatest player they ever saw play the game. Some Hall of Fame announcers have said that he was the greatest player they ever saw, excluding Ruth and other players before their time.

Willie owned the Polo Grounds as far as the Giants fans were concerned, and his address might just as well have been 155th Street and River Avenue. He made that great basket catch off a ball hit by Vic Wertz in the opening game of the 1954 World Series. We lost that series in four straight games. Bob Lemon lost that particular game in the tenth inning when Dusty Rhodes hit a home run with the score tied and two men on base.

Willie was a great base runner and a great home run hitter. He lost a couple of years due to military service, and if it were not for those lost years he certainly would have broken Ruth's record with well over 700 home runs. I would have to say Mays is one of the most popular players of all time. Leo Durocher loved him as both a player and a person. The entire baseball world liked Mays and still does today. He might well have been the best center fielder in New York, and I'm sure the New York fans will keep debating who was the best center fielder well into the millennium.

Willie's lifetime 660 home runs, 3,283 lifetime hits, 2,062 runs scored, 1,903 RBIs, and .302 lifetime batting average place him atop many categories. The numbers are truly impressive because they are all major categories, and what is also impressive are his 338 lifetime stolen bases. This is most interesting because Willie was a 300–300 club member (300 home runs and 300 stolen bases) during an era when the stolen base was used as part of the in-game strategy, not just to compile higher stats for free agents. Willie stole bases when the team was down to keep a possible victory in reach. In my day, the stolen base was used sparingly. Players did not take off and run to steal a base in a 10–0 blowout for their own personal statistics. Willie's 338 stolen bases all meant something regarding the outcome of a game.

He is truly a baseball great in every respect. Although I was on the losing side of the 1954 World Series when the Giants beat us in four straight, I'm glad that Willie had such a wonderful career in baseball.

Stan "The Man" Musial

A dear friend of mine, Stan gets my vote as the best National League ballplayer in the last century!

I was broadcasting the game between the St. Louis Cardinals and the Chicago Cubs in 1958 for "Mutual Game of the Day" when Stan got his 3,000th hit. It was a privilege to sit up in the broadcast booth and see that sweet swing swat the ball to left field for hit number 3,000. He pinch-hit in Chicago that day and sent a two-base hit to left field. Freddy Hutchinson, the manager of the Cardinals, ran out onto the field and retrieved the ball with the help of the umpires and presented it to Stan. He was replaced in the game by a pinch-runner.

As a player, Stan was one of the greatest in the National League—or in either league for that matter. I pitched against Stan in All-Star games, and he had fair success against me. My scouting report on Stan is as follows: He had an unusual batting stance, but was an exceptional hitter. He didn't have much of an arm; he started his career as a pitcher and hurt his arm, then moved to the outfield and came up through the ranks as an outfielder, finishing his career at first base. He was a great base runner, and when you combined his base running ability with his exceptional skill at the plate, then you suddenly realized how vital he was as a drawing card for the Cardinals and for the entire National League!

Stan Musial was a three-time MVP and a seven-time batting champion, and compiled some of the most impressive numbers in categories that really tell much about a hitter. He finished his career with a lifetime .331 batting average. His lifetime slugging percentage was .559, and his on-base percentage was .418. He compiled 3,630 hits and 475 home runs. He finished his career with a total of 1,949 runs scored and 1,951 runs batted in, and had eleven seasons of 100 or more runs scored and ten seasons of 100 or more RBIs in a single season. He also had 200 hits in a single season seven times in his career. Stan was The Man when it came to hitting, and his nickname was most true of his prowess at the plate.

As a person, Stan had not, and still has not, one enemy in the world. I enjoy seeing him and his wife, Lil, on cruises and at the Hall of Fame induction weekends. Stan not only played a mean harmonica, but he played the "meanest" bat around during my era.

My Friend, Satchel Paige

Satchel Paige was one of the top five or ten pitchers in the entire history of baseball in my opinion. He was someone very special to me.

I knew Satchel even before I got to Cleveland. I had pitched against him as a sixteen-year-old kid in Des Moines, Iowa. I saw Satchel pitch for the Kansas City Monarchs and for the Pittsburgh Crawfords in 1936. I pitched against him in some exhibition games on the West Coast, and after World War II his off-season, traveling all-star team played against mine. It was a great rivalry, and we had lots of fun. We traveled in two DC-3s across the United States in 1946. We had to play above the Mason-Dixon line. We could not play in Louisville, Kentucky, nor could we play in Phoenix. We could play in Cincinnati, St. Louis, and Kansas City.

My friend, Wilky Wilkinson, president of the Kansas City Monarchs, organized the team, along with the general manager, Tom Baird. Satchel's team had their own coaches, and great players such as Ted "Double Duty" Radcliffe and stellar first baseman Buck O'Neil, who now is known by the world as one of the major historians of African American baseball history.

In 1948 Satchel was my teammate, and he won six games for us, losing only one game. I fully believe that his pitching helped us to become World Series Champions that year. Satchel won twelve games for the St. Louis Browns in 1952 at the "official" age forty-six, although he was probably older than that.

Satchel had a great fastball and a great change-up, could throw from every angle, and had perfect control. He was also a great raconteur and regaled many of us with stories involving him and other great players such as Josh Gibson and James "Cool Papa" Bell.

There was nobody better than Satchel when it came to the art of pitching, or preparation for that matter. Nobody did their homework so well. He knew the scouting report on everybody. He knew the hitters and their tendencies, and he could spot a hitter's weaknesses very quickly, quicker than anyone I ever knew. He was respected by everyone all over the baseball world as one of the game's greatest pitchers.

Pee Wee Reese: The Captain

Baseball lost a great shortstop and a great person in 1999 when Pee Wee Reese died. Pee Wee was a legitimate Hall of Famer and a great person. I remember him as a team leader on and off the field. You can't think of Pee Wee and not think of Brooklyn Dodgers baseball, with other greats like Pete Reiser and Ralph Branca, and managers Leo Durocher and Walter Alston. Pee Wee also bridged the gap from Brooklyn to Los Angeles and helped to preserve the Dodger baseball tradition.

Pee Wee had 2,170 lifetime hits and 232 lifetime stolen bases, in an era when the stolen base was used sparingly. Pee Wee was the team captain and leader of the 1955 World Champion Brooklyn Dodgers, and everyone liked him, from the ushers and symphony band at Ebbets Field, to fans all around the league.

Pee Wee Reese was instrumental in helping Jackie Robinson feel comfortable from a social standpoint in the majors. His gesture of putting his arm around Jackie will always be remembered as an important act done by a great person.

Phil "Scooter" Rizzuto

Phil Rizzuto is known to the whole world as Scooter. Everybody loves Phil. He had a great career as both player and broadcaster. He was a little guy who could hit, bunt, run, and play the shortstop position with much grace.

An MVP for his offensive numbers, Phil will always be remembered for his stellar defense. He could cover a lot of ground at shortstop. He had many friends, and I don't know of a single person who didn't like little Phil. I loved the guy. While I would give the nod to Lou Boudreau and Honus Wagner, I know Phil is a close second. He is a Hall of Famer in every respect, and I was so happy when the Hall finally elected him in 1994. He deserves to be in the Hall of Fame not only for his baseball playing career, but for being an ambassador of the game. He has done so much to promote the game of baseball through his various speaking engagements. I always enjoy seeing Phil and his wife, Cora, at the Hall of Fame weekends, and whenever I see him I think back to the great Yankees-Indians duels in the late 1930s and 1940s. Those games made for some great baseball history, and there was Phil at shortstop turning the double play with the utmost of ease.

Jackie Robinson: A Pioneer

Jackie could unnerve a pitcher better than anyone. I pitched against Jackie Robinson three times in Los Angeles, San Diego, and Sacramento in 1946. He had played for the Brooklyn Dodgers AAA farm club, the Montreal Royals, at the time, but was recalled by the Brooklyn Dodgers after the season of 1946. He didn't hit the high fastball too well, but did everything else well. He was a great curveball hitter and a good breaking ball hitter in general. He was an excellent second baseman and one of the best base runners of all time.

Jackie was a great athlete, as he ran track and field, played football at UCLA, and played baseball. He served in the military during World War II and served his country honorably.

It was wrong that he was kept out of the major leagues for so long, along with other great ballplayers like Monte Irvin, Josh Gibson, and Buck Leonard, who never received the opportunity to play in the majors. I barnstormed against these players, and they were all major leaguers in my book. Baseball did the right thing, but much too late. African American players should have been allowed to play in the major leagues from day one. After all, as a country we called it our national pastime. I'm glad Jackie and Larry Doby both made it to the majors and went on to have Hall of Fame careers. Jackie was a pioneer in breaking the color barrier by being the first African American major league ballplayer. He and Pee Wee Reese helped make the Brooklyn Dodgers the storied franchise it became, winning them the World Series in 1955.

What I observed most about Jackie on the base paths was not only his pure speed, but his baseball instincts. He'd get on third base, and he'd make the pitcher balk. He would drive the pitchers crazy! He was always on base and he'd upset the other ball clubs. He had problems when he came up to the majors, but he persevered and is a credit to the game of baseball.

Jackie was a friend of mine. He was a class act all the way, and it was quite enjoyable to be elected to the Hall of Fame with him in 1962.

Duke Snider: The Duke of Flatbush

People often ask me about Duke Snider. I want to say for the record that, while I admire Duke as a player and as a fellow comrade, I have no pitching stories to tell because, much to everyone's amazement, I never pitched against him. I'm often asked how this is possible since our careers were in the same era. It's because he was in the National League and I was in the American League, and the Dodgers never played the Indians in the World Series, nor did I ever pitch against him in spring training.

As a person, Duke has been the subject of much ribbing because of his aloof attitude. He had an interesting rapport with the Dodger fans. I myself loved the Dodger supporters as a National Leaguer because they were such ardent Dodger fans that they loved to root against the Yankees, and so they would go to Yankee Stadium when I pitched and vociferously cheer for the Indians. They'd sit right behind the Yankee dugout with their megaphones, and most of the quips they hollered at the Yankee players were so shocking I myself could never repeat them to either juveniles or adults.

Warren Spahn

Warren Spahn was the winningest left-handed pitcher in history, and it comes as no surprise to me, because I know

Warren Spahn quite well from my playing days. Warren had a great screwball, great stamina, and great control, and he epitomized the "dart thrower" image of the art of pitching. He is to be imitated by any aspiring young finesse-style pitcher.

As a person, he served his country well, just as he served his Braves ball club. He was given a battlefield commission at the Battle of the Bulge when his commanding officer was killed. He was in the combat engineers and was involved in many tough skirmishes. He is a true embodiment of all that is good in society and is one of the "real heroes," as he placed his life on the line for his country.

Speaking of tough skirmishes, I remember Warren in a series of tough baseball skirmishes in 1948 when Cleveland beat the Braves to win the World Series 4–2. Warren pitched very well in that series, winning one of the Braves' only two victories, and I had a chance in 1999 to reflect with Warren Spahn on that great World Series. I saw him at the All-Star game at Fenway Park and the Legends of the Twentieth Century celebration. The famous quip in my day (the 1940s and 1950s) was "Spahn and Sain and pray for rain."

Warren Spahn's lifetime numbers are a credit to this great man. He won twenty games or more in a single season thirteen times in his career! His 363 lifetime wins are the major league record for lifetime wins by a left-hander. Warren is also ranked fifth all-time among all major league pitchers in lifetime wins. His ERA was only 3.09, and that was phenomenal considering for whom he played. Warren finished in the top twenty in lifetime complete games, and in the top ten in both lifetime shutouts and lifetime innings pitched.

I know in my heart that if Warren Spahn had not lost three years to World War II, he would have easily won more than 400 ball games. He is still one of the top twenty pitchers in baseball history.

Ted Williams: The Splendid Splinter, The Thumper, The Kid

In Boston, Massachusetts, back in the 1940s and 1950s, Ted Williams graced the outfield area below what is pleasantly termed "The Green Monster." He was known to the Fenway faithful as The Kid, The Thumper, and The Splendid Splinter. I knew him as Ted Williams, good friend and confidant.

To this day, Ted is still near and dear to me. It saddens me to see this glorious figure of a man confined to a wheelchair, unable to hunt and fish and do the little things that make him such a diverse and unique person. I visit with him twice a year and talk to him at least twice a month on the telephone.

Ted tried to get Shoeless Joe Jackson into the Hall of Fame. He took up the cause because he believed that Joe

Jackson did not throw any game, as his stats indicate, and that he tried to give the money back and said that he gave it to a hospital. Ted believes in his cause, and I admire him for that as well. Even in his older years, Ted is still trying to help the game of baseball and its icons in any capacity, and the case for Joe Jackson is just another example of Ted going to bat for someone off the field, as well as driving in runs and hitting home runs on the field. Ted Williams did much for the Red Sox's Jimmy Fund and children who were ill with cancer. During his playing days, Ted gave much support to other players around the league and had many friends in the game. Every hitter sought his thoughts on hitting, trying to find out the secrets of consistency at the plate.

Ted was a great outfielder in Fenway Park, playing that Green Monster better than anyone could have played in left field. He didn't throw to the wrong base, and he had a great arm. He knew how to play a ricochet shot off the wall, catching it on the first hop and firing the ball to second base to hold a two-base hit to a single.

For me, Ted Williams was quite a challenge because I didn't have a good sinker. I had a curve, slider, and fastball, plus an average change-up. I threw change-up curveballs. I hardly ever used a change-up on a fastball. Of course, there will always be some hitters who will outsmart you or be better than you. Ted was a better low-ball hitter than a high-ball hitter, so when I pitched to him I'd try to keep the ball up and inside on him. This was so he wouldn't be able to hit the ball on the good part of his bat. The slider was the best pitch to use with him.

I could not use my fastball against him, even though I had a good fastball. It didn't matter how great it was, Ted could hit anyone's fastball out of the ballpark for a home run. You just could not throw a fastball by Ted at all. I've often summed up trying to throw a fastball to Ted Williams as follows: It was like trying to sneak a sunbeam by a rooster early in the morning. You couldn't get it by him without him crowing loud and long at 4:30 in the morning somewhere.

Ted Williams was the greatest hitter I've ever pitched to, followed by Roger Hornsby. Ted came up from Minneapolis in 1939 and in 1941 hit .406. He served in the military in World War II and again in Korea. If it were not for all of the lost time due to military service, nobody would be near him in many categories. He would hold the record for walks, home runs, runs scored, and runs batted in, but he knew that his duty was to serve his country. When you reflect on his stats, you see how staggering his lifetime numbers are, and what could have been if not for the loss of playing time in his prime years.

Ted finished his career second all-time in slugging percentage at .634, next to only Babe Ruth. Ted ranks fifteenth all-time in lifetime on-base percentage at .413, and his lifetime batting average of .344 ranks him sixth all-time. In the categories of walks (2,019) and RBIs (1,839), Ted ranks second and eleventh, respectively. In addition to his 521 lifetime home runs, Ted scored 100 or more runs in a single season nine times in his illustrious career. Ted was a two-time American League Most Valuable Player and a two-time Triple Crown winner. His accolades were well deserved in every respect, and that is why he is a major Hall of Famer in my book.

Bill Veeck

Bill came to Cleveland in June of 1946, and he was the one who acquired Larry Doby from the Newark Eagles. Bill was great to everyone and he really enjoyed people. He was a magnet for attention because of his gregarious nature.

Bill was also very lucky in that many of his players had career years just two years after he bought the ball club. The year 1948 was the big stat year for many of the Indians players. Bill's father knew the game of baseball and passed his knowledge on to his son, as well as the knack for promoting the game. Bill's father was the CEO of the Chicago Cubs.

Bill knew the game of baseball from a promotions standpoint better than most people. Everybody liked Bill because he was not greedy for money. Ballplayers loved him because of his genuine attitude. You knew who the real Bill Veeck was, and he was honest with his players. I myself liked Bill Veeck. We never had an argument about salary in all of our years with the Indians. I thought he was a great promoter and helped promote the game of baseball well. He always had a flair for showmanship. He enjoyed "events" and was a fan of the circus. In fact, he used to follow the Ringling Brothers circus around, and he ended up marrying one of their horseback riders. Her maiden name was Raymond. They got divorced, however, and he later remarried.

I think this step in his life was an important one for Bill, as he married Mary Francis Ackerman, who was a publicity director for the Ice Capades. I say that this was an important step because a good marriage is important in anyone's life. Mary was a wonderful woman who was very good for Bill. He needed somebody like her. She was a great person, a great mother, and a wonderful wife, and she was exactly the type of woman Bill needed in his life. Her personality had a calming effect on Bill, but he was as ingenious as ever in his marketing strategies. I knew Mary Francis Ackerman three or four years before Bill met her, and let me say that he was very lucky to marry her.

Bill's one faux pas, in my opinion, was sending Eddie Gaedel, the midget, up to the plate while he owned the St. Louis Browns, after he had left the Indians. His team could not compete with the beer magnate–owned St. Louis Cardinals, and the crosstown rivalry was intense. Bill had to try something, and so he sent Eddie Gaedel up to the plate. This one act caused Bill to be unofficially banned from baseball for some time. There was a gentleman's agreement between the owners, and Bill was subtly taken out of baseball.

Bill came roaring back, however, and won the pennant many years later with the Chicago White Sox. He had flagpole sitters and cold ice giveaways. He would even bring orchids from Hawaii and place them around the necks of all the women on Ladies Day.

Bill Veeck was a writer's best friend. He was truly great for the beat writers. He'd stay up until all hours of the night talking with them. He'd stop at every bar on the way to a speech and he'd stop back at three or four bars on the way home. He'd meet and greet fans and was loved by the news media. He was great for baseball.

Breaking Records

Time takes care of everything. The good. The bad. The indifferent. Even baseball records.

I first pitched against Lou Gehrig in late August 1936. Three years later, I saw him leave the Yankees in Cleveland that fateful day in 1939 to go to the Mayo Clinic to see Dr. O'Leary. My father had been going to the Mayo Clinic since the fall of 1936 for treatment for an inoperable brain tumor, which finally caused his death in 1943. I met Dr. O'Leary three years before Lou died.

Lou Gehrig was known by all as the Iron Horse, and at the time the talk was that his consecutive games played streak would never be broken. Everyone in baseball was quite positive that for someone to break the record he would have to stay healthy and play every day for seventeen years. It seemed too much of a Herculean task. Cal Ripken Jr. accomplished the unimaginable. He stayed healthy and played every day for seventeen-plus years! The year 1996 was a poignant one, as I saw the record of someone whom I admired fall.

However, I have always believed all records were made to be broken, even DiMaggio's 56-game hitting streak. I pitched the only opening day no-hitter in history in 1940 and everyone back then said it would never be broken. I know better. Of course, it will. It's just a matter of time.

My scouting report on Gehrig went as follows: Gehrig was very strong and had great power. He was a high-ball hitter; he liked his pitches high in the strike zone. He didn't like the overhand curveball very much. He hit line drives that were vicious. He had a knack of consistently being able to hit to left-center field. As a fielder, he was an excellent first baseman. He could cover a lot of ground. I know the story that they tell about Wally Pipp telling Miller Huggins that he didn't feel well so he rested one day—and forever after, as far as the Yankees were concerned, because Lou Gehrig made his big league debut with a splash that day. Gehrig hit one home run off me and his homer tied the score in the bottom of the ninth inning with two outs. However, Cleveland won it in the tenth inning on a home run, so I was off the hook.

Gehrig had always been in the shadow of Babe Ruth, and that was because of Ruth's home runs. As I said, Gehrig was a line drive hitter, whereas Ruth would hit those high fly balls that had so much backspin on them that they would carry forever. Lou Gehrig ranks, in my book, as one of the greatest players of all time. His career batting average, to be precise, was .340, tying him with the great George Sisler on the all-time list. He compiled 200 hits or more in a single season eight times in his career. His career on-base percentage was .447 and his career slugging percentage .632, ranking him third in that category behind only Babe Ruth himself and Ted Williams, who had career slugging percentages of .690 and .634, respectively. He compiled 2,721 hits and 493 home runs before having to suddenly and tragically retire from the game of baseball with a disease that has since become known as ALS, or Lou Gehrig's disease.

I myself, on October 28, 1928, had obtained an autographed baseball that bore the signatures of both Lou Gehrig and Babe Ruth, from when they traveled through Iowa in the off-season and played an exhibition game at the Des Moines Demons ballpark. The Babe pitched one inning that game and he and Gehrig had a hitting exhibition prior to the game that rivaled any batting practice home run contest. They donned uniforms and arranged for uniforms for the local semipro players. They put on a great show for all of us in the grandstands. Babe's team was called the Bustin' Babes and Lou Gehrig's team was called the Larapin Lous. It was a treat for me at age ten to see the great Lou Gehrig, and I enjoyed following his career via the newspapers and eventually pitching against him as a young pitcher.

The Best Managers

My first manager was Steve O'Neill, who had been the catcher for the 1920 World Champion Cleveland Indians club. Steve caught for me the first inning during an exhibition game against the St. Louis Cardinals in 1936 before I joined the Indians. He was a good family man and a great person.

Lou Boudreau did not overmanage when he was a player-manager. Many managers overmanage because they are expected to change pitchers and rearrange the lineup or rotation. After all, they are supposed to manage. Even if something works, they want to fix it. Leo Durocher didn't employ that philosophy, nor did Lou.

I thought Joe McCarthy was a great manager. He liked me, and I liked him. I thought he did a great job managing the Yankees. Of course, he had great ballplayers playing for him. Most managers who are successful have the talent on the field who make them proud.

Bill McKechnie was another great manager, as was Al Lopez. In fact, I pitched to Al when Al came to Cleveland at the end of his playing career. Sparky Anderson is a great manager I would also like to mention, although he was well after my time. Sparky is now a member of the Hall of Fame, as of 2000, and rightfully so!

Umpires

Umpiring has become a subject of great controversy nowadays. Years ago, the strike zone was defined. The pitcher knew the strike zone, and so did the hitter. The base umpiring is good today, but the balls and strikes calls are lacking. Umpires today have few guidelines. Their strike zone is what they decide it is. Sometimes it's as if the factors for determining strikes include what time of day it is, how many people are on base, what town you're in, who the hitter is, who the pitcher is, what the score is, what time your dinner date is, and what time the plane is going to leave. A great umpire is someone whom the hitter and pitcher can depend on for consistency. They are finally getting better after being very inconsistent for awhile.

The great umpires I would like to mention whom I admired from my day were Bill McGowan, Bill Dineen, Cal Hubbard, Bill Klem, Jocko Conlan, and Red Ormsby. These men were just plain better. They were trained better and they were great.

Umpire supervision used to be great. Since 1999, it's been getting better. Umpires are getting better at overruling each other, and that's good for the game of baseball. A good umpire call is one that the pitcher, the hitter, and the catcher all know before it's made.

The Great Rivalries

Today, fans are entitled to the geographic feat of coast-to-coast baseball, thanks to the "jet age." You have the Giants and Dodgers on the West Coast and the East Coast rivalries such as the Yankees and Red Sox, not to mention interleague play between the Yankees and Mets, Cubs and White Sox, Indians and Reds.

The great rivalries were great for baseball: Yankees and Indians, Yankees and Red Sox, Dodgers and Giants, Yankees and Dodgers, Indians and Tigers, and Cardinals and Cubs. Rivalries today are not as ardent as they were years ago because fans know that sports is such a big business you can't take it too seriously.

Interleague play has made for some new rivalries, such as Reds and Indians and Marlins and Devil Rays. In college sports, the Big Ten, the Big Eight, and the Ivy Leagues have some great rivalries that are becoming known nationwide through television and marketing. High schools have always had rivalries, and they also are more well-known.

Even in golf there is much rivalry between players. Basketball and football have developed some great rivalries. In my day in college football Notre Dame had a rivalry with just about every other team in the country because they were so well respected as a school.

Stolen Bases

I've seen some of the greatest base stealers of all time, including Rickey Henderson of today. Max Carey was a good base stealer, as was Ben Chapman. Lou Brock was an excellent base stealer. Willie Mays stole 338 bases during his career.

My approach for base stealers as a pitcher was to step on and off the rubber and try to break their timing of my delivery. Years ago, they would steal bases only to affect the outcome of the game by advancing runners into scoring position. Base-stealing is used in many more situations today. Now they steal bases just to build up statistics to use during their free agency or salary negotiations. The statistics are much more important now than they were during my time, so it is increasingly more important for a base stealer to build up his totals each year.

Broadcasting Baseball

Ever since Ronald Reagan read the ticker tape, fans have been intrigued by the art of broadcasting. I use the word "art" because broadcasting baseball is an art. Years ago, when all that was technologically available was the ticker tape, the announcers bore the insurmountable task of having to re-create events leading up to the final outcome. The telegrapher would hand Ronald Reagan the ticker tape which read "S1S" (which meant "strike one, swinging"). It was then up to the crafty and articulate Reagan to narrate the events and to build the drama for fans listening to the Chicago Cubs game. He would have to make up the intricate details of the game. If there was a base hit to left field that should have been a double, it was up to the announcer to tell the fans that the ball went into left field and bounced off the Sherwin-Williams sign, and that the outfielder held the runner to a single by way of a beautiful throw. The announcers used to shake tin cans to synthesize "fan noise," and the tap of a pencil on the microphone would be used to simulate the ball hitting the bat.

Today, every broadcaster has his own call, such as, "It's outta here!" or "It's yard!" The expressions mean nothing, but they are the modern version of excitement and become the broadcasters' trademarks. Even in a 15–2 blowout, you must maintain your excitement for your sponsors. Most broadcasters start by broadcasting baseball in the minor leagues. I broadcast a 154-game schedule for "Mutual Game of the Day" in 1958, plus eight spring training games and playoff games. My most memorable broadcast was the day of Stan Musial's 3,000th hit in 1958, and that tape is in the National Baseball Hall of Fame in Cooperstown, New York.

My Wheaties Days

Getting on the front of a Wheaties box is a child's dream. It symbolizes the recognition of the general public that you're a star. I never dreamed, when I signed my professional baseball contract at age sixteen, that I would ever be on a Wheaties box, even though I had eaten lots of Wheaties as a young boy. I used to listen to Jack Armstrong, the all-American boy who promoted Wheaties on the radio.

In fact, I was fortunate enough to appear on Wheaties boxes many times in my career, even in pictures taken in Norfolk, Virginia, during World War II in my navy uniform. General Mills had to get permission from the navy (which they did) to use the photo.

General Mills has been manufacturing its legendary breakfast cereal since I was a kid. I vividly remember those radio commercials, announced by Ronald Reagan on WHO. Back then, Reagan would broadcast the Cubs games off the ticker tape for General Mills and I, being an impressionable child on an Iowa farm, would eat my Wheaties without ever thinking I would be on the box someday. I ended up meeting Ronald Reagan in Des Moines long before the start of his acting career in Hollywood and his political fame. He was a great president and communicator, and I'm proud to say he was a very good friend of mine.

I signed a contract with General Mills the same year that Shirley Temple did. She got $10,000 and I got $2,500.

Of course, I wasn't cute, I couldn't sing or tap dance, and I didn't have curly hair. But I was happy with my contract, nonetheless. The company kept sending checks to my mother while my father was dying of brain cancer and I was away in the navy, which I deeply appreciated.

Wheaties boxes have bridged the gap between generations. They have pictured greats from Babe Ruth, Joe DiMaggio, and Arnold Palmer to Michael Jordan and Ken Griffey Jr. For years, Wheaties has made an association between breakfast and professional sports, showing that even something nutritious can be enjoyable.

To this day General Mills is a great company, very supportive of sports and athletics, particularly baseball and basketball. I congratulate them on the contributions they have made to the game of baseball and to my own family.

My Own Candy Bar

Baseball cards were packaged with bubble gum long before I entered the baseball scene as a young lad. I was fortunate enough to have my own candy bar before World War II. It was very good and a lot of fun for me. To have your photo and statistics on a baseball card was terrific, but to have a candy bar named after you placed you in an elite category. This was every kid's dream.

The Bob Feller Bar was manufactured by the Euclid Candy Company in Brooklyn, New York. The owner of the company was from Cleveland, where the main thoroughfare was Euclid Avenue. They were manufacturing the Love Nest Bar, and they changed the cover and sold the bars as the Bob Feller Bar. The bar was similar to the Baby Ruth bar, only larger. It had a chewy center of caramel and peanuts, covered in chocolate.

I had always been intrigued by the confusion over the Baby Ruth Bar, which everyone thought was Babe Ruth's candy bar, but it was actually named for a president's daughter. Babe never saw a dime from that candy bar because the name was copyrighted before he became a baseball player.

Of course, many ballplayers have had their names on candy bars and other snacks, but my bar sold well. Even the ushers at Municipal Stadium wore caps with my name on them, selling the Bob Feller Bar for 5 cents. It was a large bar as well, so the fans got their money's worth. Nowadays, candy bars cost about fifteen times that.

I was so proud of my candy bar that I still have the wrapper and usher caps in my museum in Iowa.

I Knew Them Well

Baseball afforded me the opportunity to mingle with some high-society crowds. From politics to Hollywood, and from baseball to other sports, I met many of the stars during the 1930s, 1940s, and 1950s and knew them well.

I was privileged to get to know some presidents. I met President Eisenhower during my playing days. President Nixon was a very good friend of mine, and I think he was a good president. I know President Bush and his son George W. Bush.

I knew the Hollywood crowd and shook hands with all of them. Ronald Reagan I knew well. George Raft was a baseball fan. Donna Reed was from my home state of Iowa. Frank Sinatra, Dean Martin, and Clark Gable were other stars I became friendly with through my success in baseball. Bing Crosby and Bob Hope I got to know very well, and there were many other stars I became friendly with, but the whole point is that baseball gave me the chance to have friends who were at the pinnacle of their success in other walks of life. Without baseball, I would not have met these great people.

My Love of Flying Planes

The concept of flying was one that I became enamored with quite early in my youth. I liked flying, and that was my little adventure away from the game of baseball.

I took my first flying lessons in an old Stinson, back in a cornfield. Then I flew the PT-17 and PT-19 before the war. I bought a Fairchild and sold it just after the bombing of Pearl Harbor. I took a refresher course courtesy of the GI Bill after I was discharged from the navy, and bought my first Beachcraft Bonanza #13. I knew the Beachcraft people, Walter Beach and his wife, Olive, in Wichita. It was a great aircraft and had the V-tail, which was very unusual at the time.

Memorable Sponsorships

When I left the game of baseball in 1956, I felt satisfied with my career in the big leagues and with the fact that I would have new endeavors ahead of me. I knew that I had given 100 percent every time I had taken the pitcher's mound. I also knew that my many fans appreciated my efforts.

After my retirement, I decided I would take advantage of some sponsorship opportunities. I had a good job with the Motorola Corporation, promoting consumer products such as radios and television sets. Motorola was founded by Paul Galvin, who invented the automobile radio; the first such radio is still in their factory in Chicago.

Bob Galvin, Paul Galvin's son, was a great sports fan. The endorsements afforded me opportunities for numerous television and radio appearances. Bob wanted a national tour for the company, and he wanted his products marketed by famous athletes, particularly from baseball and football. Bob hired Otto Graham from the Cleveland

Browns for football promotions, and I did the baseball bit. I traveled all over the country, sometimes in my own aircraft, a Beachcraft Bonanza. I traveled through 44 states and 110 cities, giving away 220,000 baseballs and more than one million books on how to play the game. I would don my old uniform and give instruction to young people, which was a lot of fun.

I entered the broadcasting scene for "Mutual Game of the Day" in 1958. One sponsorship lasted for ten years. Ivan Combe from Iowa founded Combe Incorporated in Westchester, New York. He invented Grecian Formula 16, Odor Eaters, Clearasil, Sulfadine, Lanacane, and other products for people and dogs alike. They call them personal care items. Ivan died early in 2000 at age eighty-nine, and his son still runs the company in Westchester.

I also worked for Sheraton Hotels as director of sports sales for five years and for Hilton Hotels as Director of Sports Sales for five years under Baron Hilton, son of the founder and owner of Hilton Hotels, Conrad Hilton. I booked baseball and football teams into the hotels. The hotel industry is interesting because there is always something happening, 365 days a year.

I enjoyed every minute of the travel and entertainment opportunities, and I thank baseball for affording me the opportunity to have fun even after my playing career was over.

My Statue at Jacob's Field

My statue is located outside the center field wall on Ninth Street between Prospect and Carnegie Avenue in the concourse area of Jacobs Field. It has become a meeting place for fans, and that alone fills me with much joy. The statue was unveiled April 1, 1994, the day before Jacobs Field opened its doors to the baseball world for an exhibition game between the Cleveland Indians and the Pittsburgh Pirates. My wife, Anne, her daughter, Rachel, and my son, Steve, attended the unveiling.

I'm very proud of that statue—it's nice to be immortalized while you're still alive. I wish to thank national anthem singer Rocco Scottie, sculptor Gary Ross, former Indians owner Richard Jacobs, Society of American Baseball Research (SABR) president Morris Eckhouse, talkshow host John Lannigan, Indians vice president of public relations Bob DiBiasio, and everyone involved for allowing me to be honored in such a way. I deeply appreciate it. Gary did a very fine job!

PART III

Building Good Players

How to Be a Successful Pitcher

Everybody asks me this question: Do you have to be blessed and born with a good arm? I see a lot of advertising on how to pick up five or ten miles per hour on a fastball by going to a certain clinic. Not true! It's a lot of malarkey. If you can't hit a fastball the day you're born, you'll never hit one. You can learn how to throw a breaking ball or how to hit a breaking ball, but you can't learn how to hit a fastball. You might be able to tinker with your motion to throw a ball a mile per hour faster, but that's it. All of these ads are useless. You can learn control and how to pitch, but not how to throw several miles per hour faster.

The most important part of being a successful pitcher is being able to pace yourself and have stamina. To stay even or ahead of the hitter because pitchers who pitch from behind in the count are rarely, if ever, successful. To not bear down on every hitter after you get two men out and have a little lead. You need to save a little for the heart of the batting order or for the seventh, eighth, and ninth innings.

Pitchers don't do that today. They haven't the slightest idea of what you're talking about when you go over and tell them that they should pace themselves during the course of a nine-inning ball game. Pacing yourself and having control go hand in hand. If you have speed and control, you're going to be a winning pitcher, even though you don't throw 100 mph. You might have a great deal of power, but if you don't pace yourself, you may tire out on a hot day and not have the stamina to finish the ball game. I used to pace myself, and if I was ahead in the game and it was not a close game, I'd ease up and save some stuff for the seventh, eighth, and ninth innings.

Successful pitching does not hinge on speed. The movement of a pitcher's pitches is important. Sandy Koufax had great movement on his fastball, as did Herb Score and Steve Carlton.

A pitcher should also protect himself as a fielder. Always keep your glove ahead of your elbow when you make your delivery so you can protect the upper half of your body if a bullet is hit through the box. Herb Score got hit in the eye by a line drive off the bat of Gil McDougald and was never the same. If Herb had protected himself, he might have been able to deflect the ball, and would have gone on to become one of the greatest pitchers of all time with the stuff he had at that time. It's much easier said than done, however.

Pitchers should also practice control and pitch batting practice, as well as do lots of long runs to build up stamina. Stay ahead of the hitter. Throw strikes. Don't try to pitch from behind. If you do, you'll be giving in to the hitter and you'll end up giving him his pitch. You need to throw what you want when you want to throw it. If you're a two-pitch pitcher like Sandy Koufax, who had a great fastball and curveball, then develop those pitches thoroughly. A pitcher who is a two-pitch pitcher is in good shape, as long as those two pitches are great. A three-pitch pitcher is in the best shape because he has that one extra pitch to rely on in key situations. Walter Johnson, however, became a Hall of Famer as a one-pitch pitcher. He only had the fastball.

The Things Pitchers Should Know

If you don't have a great arm, you can only improve your fastball one or two miles per hour, in spite of all of the stories you might read about in advertisements. I've seen these ads and heard coaches tell pitchers they can drastically improve their fastball and gain speed by tinkering with the way they shove off the mound or how they bend their elbow. Usually these "coaches" are the ones who never got too far in the game themselves. You cannot teach a pitcher how to throw a fastball, and this is something that every pitcher should know. Pitchers should always keep their glove in front of their elbow when they make their delivery to protect the upper part of the body in case a hitter hits a bullet back through the box. If you don't, there's no way to protect your face.

Always stay ahead of the hitter. If you don't, he'll end up having the advantage.

Know how to warm up before a ball game. Know the weather conditions and how you feel, and remember not to leave all your stuff in the bullpen or on the sidelines. Save your best stuff for the game.

Know how to back up bases and hold the runners on base. Pitchers need to know how to hold men on base without throwing to first. For instance, a pitcher can look over to first base three or four times and then step off. Know the second-base pickoff play. Rehearse all your defensive plays after a long road trip when the team comes home. Otherwise, you'll become apprehensive and make a mistake when certain situations present themselves. Knowing what to do is very important. Being able to act on this knowledge on the next pitch is what makes the difference.

Keep books on the hitters. Plan ahead in your workouts. Write down what you're going to do the next day the night before so that you can be prepared for the game. Some players may feel that this is too arduous a task. Well, if staying in the majors or making the Hall of Fame is important to you, then I suggest you listen to my advice. Keeping a book on each team's hitters is invaluable because, even though you might still not fare that well in any one face-off with them, you will be more successful than unsuccessful. Pitchers should know the consequences of their pitching decisions, as in a chess game. Every move they make has a countermove and a consequence. If a pitcher has studied the hitters and has done his homework, then he will be successful and this may be the edge that takes a pitcher who is barely surviving and makes a bona fide major leaguer out of him—or it may elevate the superstar to Hall of Fame status. Either way, if you keep a book on your hitters, you can't lose!

Trial and Error Method

I'm often asked about the best methods by which to teach children how to play baseball. Here's my personal experience with teaching. This comes from the standpoint of me as the student, rather than me as the teacher.

I learned how to pitch by playing catch with my dad in our backyard on our farm. We used what my dad called the "trial and error method." We watched the professionals play, and I tried to emulate them. In my day, it was harder than it is today because there wasn't any television and ballparks were not as accessible. However, I would always be throwing a baseball to my father at odd moments when I wasn't at school and, after a while, I found a pitching motion that just felt comfortable and natural to me. I had become a "pitcher." Kids throw the baseball all the time, but pitching is different than throwing. Pitching involves being able to throw hard and to change speeds.

My first love in baseball, however, was not pitching but just playing any position. I wanted to play and I would play anywhere. I played shortstop, second base, and third base, and I finally turned out to be a pitcher when I was fifteen.

My father and I would even take our baseball gloves and a ball with us and play catch after dinner when we visited relatives on Sundays. It was this informal, but constant, practicing that really prepared me to be a major league baseball player. At home, especially, we always had our after-dinner catches and afternoon catches. As I said, I learned how to throw by continually doing it and developing a motion that felt comfortable. It really is, when you come down to it, the best way for a child to learn the game of baseball. Practice and have fun, and just see what comes naturally. It's all about trial and error.

My advice to dads and moms across the country is to let kids experiment with different throwing motions and different batting stances until they feel comfortable. They have to do what comes most naturally to them. They need to be comfortable to achieve good results, and they should be experimenting without any pressure! Let the kids have fun and try to play catch with them at odd intervals during the weekend, rather than for a long period once a week. Simulate swinging and pitching with a bat or ball.

The Pitcher-Catcher Relationship

I tell every young pitcher that if the catcher calls for a pitch that he doesn't feel comfortable throwing in that particular situation, he should not throw the pitch. He should throw what he wants to throw.

However, much confusion as to pitch selection can be avoided by proper pregame preparation. Before the game, a pitcher must talk with the catcher, and preferably infielders as well, about the hitters they're going to face. I always discussed the tendencies of the hitters I was going to face with my catcher and infielders at the clubhouse meeting before each series.

I would seldom shake a catcher off, maybe two or three times during a game on average. I wouldn't shake my head, but rather I'd just stand there on the mound and stare until the catcher gave me my sign. I might wiggle my glove a little bit, but that's it. By nodding your head at a catcher to shake off or accept signs, you allow the batter to guess what pitch is coming next. Big mistake. The catcher has to know what you're thinking. I've shaken catchers off and the fellows at the plate have hit balls out of the ballpark. I've also thrown the pitch that the catcher called for and the batters sent those balls into the seats faster than I could turn my head.

The personal side of the pitcher-catcher relationship often depends on the ages and the experience of both players. The young pitcher with an experienced catcher behind the plate will take the catcher's advice and throw the pitch the catcher calls for because the catcher knows the hitters better than the pitcher does. The young pitcher will vitally depend on his catcher's knowledge in order to be successful and not give the hitter the pitch he might be looking for in a given at bat.

The older pitcher has the advantage. He wants the kind of catcher who can drive in runs for him and who can throw well, to pick runners off base and keep them honest. This pitcher has the last say on the pitch because he is the one who is going to be responsible for the mistakes he makes on the mound. Some catchers are better pitch-callers than others, but it's still the pitcher's responsibility to make sure that the batter does not reach base. It's not the catcher's responsibility to get the batter out. Rollie Hemsley, Frank Hayes, Jim Hegan, Frank Pytlak, and Charlie George were several great catchers who caught many of my games.

Pitchers must keep a book on hitters. What I mean by a "book" is a physical book on each team and their hitters. A pitcher must know how successful or unsuccessful he has been against each hitter if he wants to excel in major league baseball. I also recommend that any aspiring pitchers read the box scores before they pitch. Pitchers should also watch batting practice, for it reveals many a baseball secret. That's why the scouts for each team watch batting practice. If you get to the ballpark early, you'll see the straw-brimmed hats and the team credentials being worn like necklaces at an opera. Those men are the scouts who are there not to sun themselves, but rather to soak up all of the key information that will be revealed during batting practice.

Don't blame your mistakes on the catcher. The pitcher must know who's hot and who's not. Remember the cardinal rule: a .200 hitter in a batting streak is much more dangerous than a .350 hitter who happens to be in a slump!

You, as the pitcher, have the last say and it's your call. Take charge of your game!

The Pitching Coach–Pitcher Relationship

Pitching coaches are great for the game as long as they don't overcoach. They should take into consideration the pitcher's motion and the type of pitcher he is before giving advice. I would be very careful before listening to a pitching coach who didn't pitch the same way I did. Mel Harder would be very observant. He could watch me and tell me whether or not I was in the groove.

Pitching coaches should not make the pitcher throw the way they throw, but rather the way the pitcher throws when he's at his best. If a coach observes a pitcher enough times, he'll know what that pitcher's best stuff looks like and he should have the pitcher imitate himself at that level. For instance, a pitching coach such as Mel Harder could see whether you were overstriding, whether you were taking your windup properly, or whether you were staying ahead of the hitters.

Nowadays, the pitching coach keeps books on the number of pitches a pitcher throws to indicate whether he might be tiring or nearing his limits. (Pitch count is also used when a player comes off the disabled list to prevent him from overextending himself the first time back out on the mound.) I didn't pay much attention to that at all. I was primarily concerned with how I felt that day. A pitcher can often be his own best critic. I never had a pitch count.

The Importance of Holding Men on Base

Holding men on base is vital to a pitcher's success in the major leagues. Most pitchers feel that they have to physically throw over to first base each time they want to hold a man there. This is not true. A pitcher should look runners back to the bag, taking his foot off the pitching rubber, and not throw until the runner is motionless or moving back toward first base. You can practice this either at home or in front of a mirror in your hotel room.

Road trips are just that—road trips. They are not vacations. The players should evaluate their game along the way. Road trips are an excellent opportunity to make use of time in the hotel room for pregame homework. If you lost a game, ask yourself was it because you made a mental error or was the other team just better on that particular day. There is no excuse, and I've said this before, for pitchers losing games because of improper fundamentals, especially when it comes to relaying throws, backing up the plate, throwing to the base, or covering first base. In many situations the pitcher becomes a fifth infielder and must be prepared.

Pickoff moves to second base should be coordinated in form with the shortstop. Let the shortstop give the sign. Be sure the center fielder gets the sign so that he can break at the same time as the shortstop starts to move to receive the throw. It is then up to the pitcher to throw the ball about two or three feet toward third base between the belt and the shoulders. Pitchers should not be throwing the ball around the second base bag or around the shoelaces or the knees of the shortstop. It is much easier for the shortstop to cover second base than it is for the second baseman because the runner and opposing team's first and third base coaches can see the second baseman. The runner cannot see the shortstop; only the coaches can. Many times, the coaches will yell and the interim between the yelling of the coach and the pitcher's move to second is too long for the runner to be successful in getting back to the base. Pickoff plays can be done with the third baseman, but the timing must be perfect. It must be executed on the full run, with the pitcher throwing to third base and picking off the runner.

Holding a runner on second base is crucial because it is easier for a runner to steal third base than it is for him to steal second, even though the catcher has a shorter throw to third. If a ball is hit very hard on the ground to the outfield, the pitcher will be mightily upset with himself if he did not avail himself of the opportunity to pick off a runner or hold him near the base before delivery.

Stealing Signs: The Pitcher's Solution

The pitcher's solution to the opposition stealing signs from the dugout or from the coach's line is not to grip the ball the way he's going to throw it until he has his glove over the ball during the windup and can cover it up. Once in a while the pitcher might want to hold the ball a different way and waste a pitch if he feels that the third base or first base coach is calling his pitches. This way the batter will be circumspect about accepting a sign from either coach. As far as the runner on second base stealing signs, it's up to the pitcher and catcher to have an indicator sign and to change that indicator sign every so often. There is no excuse for allowing the hitter to know what pitch is coming. Any pitcher with a little intelligence can prevent himself from telegraphing a pitch to the batter.

Throwing Between Starts

I don't think most pitchers throw enough. It's up to the individual pitcher how much to throw. I believe pitchers should be doing long-distance throwing in spring training and during the season to strengthen their arms. Pitching during batting practice will help strengthen your arm and improve your control. In Japan pitchers would warm up 100 feet away from the catcher and then come closer. In the United States it is the opposite. Pitchers usually start throwing about 10 or 15 feet in front of the mound and then walk back to the regulation distance. After pitchers loosen themselves up with some long-distance throwing, they should take infield practice, throwing a couple of hundred feet. Once you're perspiring and properly warmed up, you can throw all out. Some coaches won't agree with me.

The day before I struck out eighteen batters, my roommate and I had a long-distance throwing contest, throwing from home plate into the left-field bleachers, which is 375 feet. Evidently it stretched out my arm pretty well!

I fully believe in long-distance throwing and infield practice for pitchers although many managers disagree with me. If I were a manager, I'd insist on this point. I used to pitch batting practice on my middle day during the rotation, and would still pitch with three days' rest. I didn't throw much before the game, but I did wind sprints between starts.

The Weight Rooms

You don't need to be a Santa Monica Beach Adonis who looks like the front cover model for *Muscle & Fitness* magazine. It's not advantageous to become so muscular that you can't bend your elbow back far enough to give your ear a gentle tug. In the game of baseball, when players get musclebound, they get injured. You need to use common sense when it comes to weights.

Weight training is important in baseball. I've always used weights, and have always done physical exercise. I believe in the philosophy that you shouldn't build up big biceps or big muscles in your body or in your legs. You need long, lean muscles. Therefore, you shouldn't use heavy weights. Players shouldn't be trying to lift very heavy weights—not more than 125 lbs, and for dumbbells not more than 10, 15, or 25 lbs. Players should use the medicine ball and the rowing machine, but should not build up muscles to the point where they can't bend their arms anymore. I've hit a speed bag, which is also useful. The triceps are just one of the muscle groups that are needed to pitch effectively, as are the extender muscles.

Light weight training, deep knee bends, skipping rope, chin-ups, and push-ups are all part of the regimen that I practiced aboard ship during World War II, twice a day when conditions permitted me to do so. This regimen is good physical training for baseball players because it employs both cardiovascular exercise and limited weight use. The point is that once you become musclebound, your ability to throw a baseball if you're a pitcher, or to hit a baseball if you're a hitter, diminishes. Some players today are just so bulked up that it hinders their pitching delivery, and you can't tell them otherwise because these weight-lifting programs become a rather compulsive activity.

Everyone has heard of the law of diminishing returns. This adage couldn't be more true when it comes to the convergence of the game of baseball and weight training. There is a point at which you've maximized your potential and anything more is too much and consequently counterproductive.

The Importance of Teamwork

It is often said that teamwork is the most important ingredient in winning a baseball game. I find that teamwork is essential for everything in life: from winning ball games, to winning real wars, to having a lasting relationship with a friend or a lasting marriage.

I've mentioned my undying love for my parents and my desire to help with our daily chores on our farm in Iowa. Teamwork was what enabled our family to prosper, and it was why my field of dreams was built. It was also why America emerged victorious from World War II.

I'll never forget my first "live" example of teamwork during World War II. We were sitting in Iceland, at Reykjavik Harbor, and we heard on radio that the Nazis were decorating a German sub commander for sinking the carrier *Ranger*. We were sitting in the harbor and the *Ranger* was sitting right beside us! This taught me that everyone was trying to use the concept of teamwork for their own advantage. That decoration ceremony was all propaganda. The same thing occurred in the Pacific when Tokyo Rose was on every night telling us what they were going to do to the Third Fleet and Task Force 58. They said that they knew where we were. Of course, they knew where we were. We knew where they were as well, but there was one thing we had that they did not have: teamwork.

I joined the navy in Norfolk after being sworn in on December 10, 1941—three days after Pearl Harbor. My high-frequency hearing loss prevented me from becoming a pilot, which saddened me, as I enjoyed flying. After attending war college in Newport, Rhode Island, I was assigned to the battleship USS *Alabama* shortly after it was commissioned in Hampton Roads. I was an antiaircraft gun captain on a 40-millimeter quad in the Pacific. The *Alabama* went to the Pacific along with the battleship *South Dakota* and other auxiliary vessels.

Our captains and admirals gave us great leadership and showed us a paradigm of teamwork. Even during recreation, we had excellent teamwork. We played catch and softball aboard our battleship. The Sea Bees would build ball diamonds on the islands we took over in the South Pacific, after our bombardment, and we'd use the diamonds to play baseball. We would resupply, lick our wounds, and then go and take another island. It usually took a month to capture an island, sometimes two months, but we had excellent teamwork, so we emerged victorious at each encounter.

Teamwork is best taught through good leadership. Good leaders foster cohesive teamwork. We need men like General Dwight Eisenhower, General Douglas MacArthur, General George Patton, General Colin Powell, and Admiral Chester Nimitz.

What does this have to do with baseball wisdom? Everything. My exposure to real live World War II battles taught me, just as I'm telling all of you now, that teamwork has much to do with victory. Teamwork is not telling the Little Leaguers that they must act like soldiers. It is a concept based upon which children should pull together and help one another, and upon which coaches should build a sense of community through sports. I've used the military examples of teamwork to show how in all walks of life the concept of community is important.

In sports, teamwork should enable all members of the team to play together and to be friends! Kids should have *fun* with baseball. It is a kid's game, after all.

The 1948 Cleveland Indians won the World Series because of teamwork. Satchel Paige pitched well the whole year. Steve Gromek and Bob Lemon were great in the stretch. Larry Doby made for a great offense, and the other players rallied behind him. Lou Boudreau and Kenny Keltner were great. Several other players with career years were also great in the stretch. The 1998 Yankees won because of teamwork. No team wins a World Series because of any one individual, but rather through the efforts of an entire team. Just look at the heroes in the World Series. Many times they are not the $10,000,000 players. You need an entire team to win the World Series, at any level, whether it be Little League or major league. Parents should teach the concept of teamwork to their children at the earliest stages of life. It will be one of the most important lessons they teach.

Confidence

Confidence is usually built by taking care of yourself and by being satisfied with your lifestyle. You need to get your rest and eat properly. A pitcher must plan ahead, practice, and work hard—no dissipation. I've always lived by the adage that an hour of sleep before midnight is worth two hours of sleep after midnight.

The most important lesson I learned in baseball, as well as in my wartime experience, was the importance of hard work and planning ahead. You need to check out your opposition in order to compete effectively. If you are confident about working harder than your competition, you are going to have a better chance of winning. If you've shirked your duty, you'll choke or flinch. You need to walk out to the pitcher's mound with the utmost confidence, tell yourself that you are in charge, and then take charge. If you get knocked out, then so be it. Come out next time and try it again. If you're fully prepared, then you won't flinch when it comes down to the tight spots, the little things that are so important and happen throughout a ball game. Simply put, a pitcher must have intelligence.

You can't teach intelligence. Education and intelligence don't have too much to do with each other. Just because you're educated doesn't mean you're smart. Anybody can read a book. You have to put it all together, take a look around, see what your decision is, and then stick to it. Confidence comes from your take-charge attitude after you're satisfied that you have prepared yourself to the fullest extent possible.

Games are won or lost in the mind, not on the mound!

Good Sportsmanship Defined

Good sportsmanship is being a decent human being. Good sportsmanship is giving credit where credit is due.

Be polite to the fans and accept accolades graciously! You are always going to meet somebody a little bit better than you are in most any walk of life. No matter how far you go, or how high you rise, or how much success you have, you will almost always run into somebody a little smarter, a little stronger, and a little better than you who does the job better and works harder.

It's analogous to being on the All-Star team in the state of Iowa. Then the question is are you the best player in your county? If so, are you the best player in the conference? The best player in the state? The best in the United States? The best in the world? There will always be someone better, and sportsmanship is giving that person his or her due credit in being better, as there is always room for improvement.

Good sportsmanship is also playing within the rules. In baseball, I've seen some examples of great sportsmanship and some examples of poor sportsmanship. In the latter case, the "headhunters" who are out there on the mound bother me. Baseball doesn't need headhunters; I think that's ridiculous. I never threw at anybody. I hit a few people, but never intentionally. I've seen some nasty plays at second base that I don't like either. If a base runner is going to be out at second base by ten feet and then goes in hard and throws a block into the second baseman or shortstop covering second base, I think that's poor sportsmanship if the play is already over. If a base runner slides hard to break up a double play, that's one thing, but if his intention is merely to slide spikes high to injure the opponent's second baseman, then that falls within the confines of my definition of poor sportsmanship.

Good sportsmanship is not breaking the rules or cheating to win. A baseball game is not a war. Any coach or manager who tells his players that they're going to play the game like they're fighting a war has never been in a war. I've been in a real war, World War II, and believe me, it's completely different.

Recipe for a Good Life in Baseball

1. Stay in general good health.
2. Observe proper nutrition.
3. Stay off the booze.
4. Don't do drugs.
5. Get enough sleep the night before you play.
6. Exercise all year round.

PART IV

Philosophies on Baseball and Life

Teaching Baseball Fundamentals

Baseball fundamentals are an important part of a team's success and camaraderie. Sad to say, teams don't practice that many fundamentals anymore.

Pitchers should back up the bases. They should be able to grab a cutoff throw and throw to the base without throwing down the left or right field line or into the dugout, allowing a run to score. In my days, the pitchers had infield practice; they were forced to throw the ball around the infield. Even in Japan they keep that tradition. The coaches in Japan teach their players to hit the cutoff man. Here, many a ball game has been lost in a rather disgusting manner by a pitcher making a fielding error. I've seen many games where pitchers have had what I term "lapses in judgment," where they commited errors of omission, failing to react quickly enough to throw to the right base. Players don't ever play "pepper" anymore because groundskeepers think it disturbs the grass.

Fans today come to the ballpark to see home runs, so that's where the big money is. Starting pitchers and closers get paid well. Defensive players don't get paid as much as they're worth in most cases because catching ground balls or pop-ups isn't seen as important. That's also why players don't do much bunting, dragging bunts, hitting behind the runner, or stealing bases when it means something. They steal bases when they're ten runs behind or ahead to run up the numbers, and it doesn't necessarily have anything to do with winning the game. There were great base stealers years ago who stole bases to win or save games. Today, it's run, run, run, and build up the statistics.

The irony of this is that, without the fundamentals, a team isn't going to be very successful. Teams just don't teach fundamentals, and even when they do teach them in spring training, they fail to review them after road trips during the season—when it counts!

The Meaning of Spring Training

Spring training, to real baseball fans, is the harbinger of spring. Fans run to their fantasy baseball guide, look at stats, and begin to postulate. However, for the ballplayer, spring training is the time when you physically and mentally prepare yourself for the season. It has a different connotation to different players in different situations.

Until the last two weeks, a lot of spring training is only for conditioning and is highly exaggerated. It's used to hype up the sale of tickets, promote the game, and sort out the players within the organization. But it's a necessary part of baseball.

A pitcher can get in condition, if he takes care of himself, in a month. Of course, pitchers rarely pitch nine innings any more, so it takes longer to get your arm in shape. If you work out all winter, then you can get in condition in the month of spring training to be at the top of your game. It doesn't really take that long for position players to get ready, maybe three weeks.

My off-season workout program was as follows: I would do some ice skating, play as much basketball as I could, and hunt as well. I'd also play some golf, but not too much. I did a lot of running and calisthenics and practiced the fundamentals such as backing up bases, covering the bag, fielding bunts, fielding comebackers, and throwing to the bases.

The last two weeks of spring training I really bore down. I wanted my fastball, slider, curveball, and change-up to be working well, whether or not I got anybody out. The only players who really care about stats are the ones who have to get a job or the rookies trying to make the ball club. I was trying to get myself prepared for the regular season.

The teams that win a lot during spring training will usually be the worst teams in the league. They're trying to win so that they can sell tickets back home. Who wins the Grapefruit League or Cactus League Pennant has no bearing on the regular season. In fact, it may be just the reverse. The teams that play the worst during spring training may be the best ball clubs because they've already sold their tickets to the fans, win or lose.

The Meaning of Statistics

Statistics don't always tell the whole story; this has always been the axiom. The concept of statistics is a rather malleable one that can be changed to suit those doing the computing.

Statistics have to be offset against conditions, no matter what the sport. In basketball, statistics must be offset based on whether or not the court is regulation length. The same is true in hockey. In baseball, statistics are dependent on the foul lines, the fences in the outfield, and the baseball. In football, the NFL brought the hash marks in to give the runners a chance to gain more ground.

In baseball, home runs in some parks may not mean as much as home runs in other parks. Many times the rules will be changed so as to allow records to be broken. This gives more hype to the game. In the last thirty years, hype has become very important. Sports is big business nowadays, and it's not who wins, but what the bottom line will show from an economic standpoint. Statistics also allow for controversy in the papers and help promote talk shows and feature movies. Who's the best is the biggest question, alongside the debate about who should be in the Hall of

Fame. Every region and city has its favorite players and will argue about them forever.

I mention statistics for key players only because the numbers speak for themselves. These players don't need to highlight any one category because their numbers are high in many categories, creating an overall great package. Stan Musial, Ted Williams, Joe DiMaggio, Warren Spahn, Willie Mays, Mickey Mantle, and, of course, Babe Ruth were all consummate players, and statistics merely enhance their already well-known and glorious careers. I merely use the numbers to show their dominance in their respective eras. Today, statistics are much more important than they used to be, with the exception of a few vital statistics: batting average, slugging percentage, wins, and losses. This is why pitchers and hitters have many more statistical categories than when I played. It's fine with me, but as you add more categories, you also must be careful about how much emphasis should be placed on any one of these categories.

Baseball Marketing: Then and Now

Today, kids have their baseball cards, their video games, and their television shows devoted to kids and athletics. That was not the case back in my day.

Years ago, Lifebuoy soap and Wheaties signs dominated the baseball parks. Lifebuoy particularly was extremely popular. The soap was orange, and it had a tremendous amount of Lysol in it. Most ballplayers used Lifebuoy, which they received gratis, and they smelled like Lysol— even from twenty feet away! A ballplayer who had just taken a shower could be recognized at quite a distance. Eventually, the manufacturers were able to lessen the odor. Lifebuoy soap was brought here from England, where it was known as the Sunshine dog soap. The owner decided that if his soap was fit for an English dog, it should be fit for the American public. He brought it over here and became very wealthy. When they were able to extract that smell from the soap years later, I decided to agree to an endorsement opportunity with them. I made a commercial for Lifebuoy soap with my family. This was during the early 1950s when I was still a ballplayer.

Sherwin-Williams paint company is located in Cleveland, Ohio, and their signs were part of the fabric of Municipal Stadium and Jacobs Field. The company is still a proud sponsor of baseball to this very day. They are just more nationally known because of television, and there are many other advertisers to whom television has afforded great marketing opportunities.

The advent of television brought mass promotional opportunities to baseball, from clothing, to automobiles, to just about any product to which a logo can be affixed. Even the simplicity of the baseball card was elevated to mammoth marketing proportions. Baseball players, with television, received national exposure that they had not received before. In my day, you were either on the cover of *Time* or *Newsweek*, as I and other baseball icons were, or you had your picture in your local paper. The only other market for a player was through Movietone newsreels, which were out of the control of the player.

Today, card shows are prevalent all across the country and many fans come to visit with the players of their youth. Clothing manufacturers have a tremendous amount of sales from an athlete's endorsement of their product through television, particularly cable and satellite. The satellite dish also has made available games which were not available in certain regions of the country. Fans in New York can watch Cubs games and vice versa. This was not the case even ten years ago.

In my day, selling tickets at the gate generated much revenue for the ball club. Today, ticket sale revenues have been replaced with multiyear television deals. Each new age will bring new forms of marketing, and technology will govern the pace at which the fans receive the information.

Loyalty in Sports: Is There Any?

I'm often asked about "loyalty in sports," and my answer is always that today and for years to come, there will be very little because of the big business into which baseball has grown. Players, even if they want to stay and play for their home team or for a particular city, far too often are persuaded by their agents to go where the money is because the agents want more money and a larger cut of the pie. Ballplayers might have heartfelt ties to a certain city like Cleveland or New York because of friends, family, good schools for their children, or ambiance, but often the agents pull the strings and the players become marionettes.

It's show business, entertainment, and a big race for the Almighty Dollar. Loyalty in sports is just about a thing of the past, except in cases like Tony Gwynn of the San Diego Padres, whom I deeply admire; Cal Ripken Jr. with the Baltimore Orioles; or even Ken Griffey Jr., who went to the Cincinnati Reds to be with his family, which was a class act. These admirable men are not the norm, unfortunately, but the exception. Baseball should promote players who exhibit such loyalty because men like Gwynn, Ripken, and Griffey are great for the game. I don't blame the players that much, as they are all fine young men, but many have very forceful agents who end up dictating to the players instead of listening to them.

What a Ballpark Should Be

The return to the old-style ballpark is great for television and advertising. They are short and they don't have much foul territory, leaving little space for the outfielders to catch a foul ball—and for good reason. Nobody pays to see a fly ball caught in foul territory. The old ballparks, though angular, had a reasonable amount of foul territory, thus allowing the fans to be close to the action and at the same time promoting defense by giving the outfielders and infielders a chance to catch pop-ups in foul territory. Jacobs Field in Cleveland is a real state-of-the-art ballpark, seating forty-two thousand, with the appropriate amount of foul territory down the lines.

If I were designing a ballpark, I'd build one as follows: 430 feet in straightaway center field, 350 or 355 feet down the left and right field lines, and 385 or 390 feet down the power alleys. Of course, the way the ball is made now—with the thin cover, the tight winding, and the light-weight bats—the hitters are still going to send the balls out of the ballpark like rockets. I'm not merely surmising that the balls are more tightly wound than they were when I played. I *know* it because I've gripped them. When you've pitched in the big leagues as long as I did, you know the way the ball should feel and you can tell if the cover is thinner and if the seams are stitched in a tighter fashion. Now the balls are covered with cowhide, but during my career they were covered with horsehide.

Baseball is the least costly of all of the four major sports. Teams should not overcharge the fans. Parking should be reasonable in price and accessibility.

I am partial to Jacobs Field because the ballpark has been designed such that fans can go get their hot dogs and goodies and still see the game when they're away from their seats, watching it on TV monitors and hearing it on the radio. Architects have done a great job going back to the old-style ballparks. The minor leagues have some great ballparks that I recommend real baseball fans visit because the seats are close to the action, the prices are affordable, and you can catch a rising star every time you attend a game.

One Hundred Years of the American League

Since the American League was formed in 1901, the rules have stayed the same but there are certain aspects of baseball that have changed. Horsehide baseballs have yielded to cowhide balls. Baseball gloves have become larger and better, making for better defense today. Their webbed pockets have improved play tremendously. Double-knit uniforms have replaced the old heavy, flannel uniforms worn when I played. In 1936 the groundskeepers could affect the contour of the pitcher's mound. Today, the mound is uniform throughout baseball. I would like to see, however, a uniform strike zone enforced that umpires can be taught accordingly.

The American League's one hundredth birthday proves that baseball is still our national pastime and that anyone with coordination can play the game, whether they're big or small.

Cy Young and the Cy Young Award

The education of every ballplayer should encompass the history of the game. Cy Young won 511 games in his illustrious career, and finished with a 2.63 lifetime ERA. He is first all-time in wins, complete games (815), and innings pitched (6,356.2), and is in the top five in shutouts with 76. His 2,803 strikeouts rank him in the top fifteen players of all time. That's the player, Cy Young.

I never won a Cy Young Award because it was established in 1956, the year I retired. I knew Cy Young well and attended his funeral in Paoli, Ohio, about ninety miles southwest of Cleveland. Cy used to come to the ballpark a lot and would visit with me in the dugout at Municipal Stadium. We had a lot of pictures taken together, and I cherish them. Cy Young won games and was one of the original members of the Hall of Fame. He had many friends all over baseball and was a respectable man with a lot of character. He pitched during the dead ball era, as did Walter Johnson for half of his career (the live ball came out in 1920).

Some people, I know, would want me to comment on the concept of the earned run average and what I think about it. The answer is: not much. The only thing that counts is whether you win or lose. I think any pitcher who wins 300 games should win 100 more games than they lose. That's not always the case. Earned run average doesn't mean anything to me except for young players in high school, college, or the minor leagues. Wins are all that count in the majors.

At the major league level a smart pitcher will pace himself and ease up, as I often did, to allow some runs, so that he saves himself for the complete game and the win. Some pitchers who have poor seasons point to their low earned run average and say that they had a good year. If you had a great year with many wins, forget your earned run average. You won! The only time ERA does you any good is if you were unfortunate enough to lose many more games than you won in a given year, but were lucky enough to not allow many runs per game.

People ask me all the time about Cy Young Award voting and whether the number of wins should determine who receives the award or whether earned run average should be a factor. I always say that the team for which the pitcher played is a third factor which bears consideration. All three factors must be taken into account.

Interleague Play: Is It Good for Baseball?

I'm all for interleague play. I'd like to see four divisions: east, west, mid-Atlantic, and midwest, with the season cut back a few games. Some people think the wild card is important. I'm not against the wild card, but I would prefer not to have a wild card and instead have four divisions.

Interleague play in a limited amount is fine, but it must be limited so that the World Series remains the paramount goal of each team and carries the significance it has carried throughout baseball's glorious history. Some friends say that interleague play and the All-Star game belittle the World Series. Whoever wins the All-Star game, it does not necessarily mean that particular league houses the best players in the game. The All-Star game is all show business. The teams must all be represented and this places the manager at a strategic disadvantage. He may have a group of players on his team who he doesn't want because he feels that they are not the best talent in the league. To me, this belittles the All-Star game.

I am not for all-out interleague play in a more concentrated fashion. Baseball is entertainment and show business; wherever the money is, that is where the game is headed. The answers to most questions come from just following the money.

The Major League Baseball Alumni Association

I'm often asked just what the Major League Baseball Alumni Association does, and my answer is they organize personal appearances, golf tournaments, and other events, then they split the proceeds among charities. The organization has its headquarters in Colorado Springs, and its head is Dan Foster. The organization was formed by ballplayers in Washington, D.C., many years ago to foster the networking of business and baseball for charitable causes. The organization has successfully raised much revenue and has given a lot of money to help needy individuals and worthy causes.

The Creation of the Baseball Players Pension

The Major League Baseball Players Pension was started by Commissioner Happy Chandler and owner Larry Mac-Phail in the fall of 1946. Dixie Walker represented the National League and Johnny Murphy was the American League representative. About twelve players had jumped ship to the Mexican League, and Ted Williams, Joe DiMaggio, and I were asked to join the Mexican League as well. They promised us $120,000 a year for three years, all the money would be up front, and it would be placed in an American bank before we crossed the Rio Grande. In order to get the players who had left back to the United States, the commissioner decided to give them amnesty and started a pension plan for them. The more famous of these players were Sal Maglie (known as the Barber by the

Giants fans at the Polo Grounds), Mickey Owen, Junior Stevens, and Max Lanier.

The commissioner's office started the plan with $600,000 in radio rights, and the players would get 50 percent of both the major league baseball radio rights and television rights. They played more All-Star games for a few years to raise the money. The money was contributory then, but now it's noncontributory.

The pension's first attorney was J. Norman Lewis, whom I knew well in New York. Marvin Miller managed to get the club owners to agree on the subject of free agency and arbitration, and Curt Flood and Andy Messersmith were influential as well in wresting a better deal for the players from the owners. Catfish Hunter was instrumental in the process of breaking the reserve clause. The reserve clause was never intended to benefit the ballplayers at all. It was an owner's tool.

Today, the players have medical benefits, retirement benefits, insurance, dental benefits, and a full pension. The provision for a vested pension used to be five years of major league playing service. Then the rules were amended to allow for vesting of the pension after only four years. Now players vest more every day they are in a major league uniform and on a major league payroll. It's a great pension plan.

Donald Fehr runs the pension today and is doing a good job for the players. They recently increased the old-timers' benefits.

Four-Day Versus Five-Day Rotation

This has become a controversy that depends on how much stamina the pitcher has within him. I worked on a farm and was used to manual labor, so I had a lot of stamina. There is no reason why a pitcher without an injury cannot pitch with three days' rest. I don't believe in five-day rotations. Nowadays, it seems like that is it. Call it a custom or a fad, but I am not very happy with the situation. I know Billy Martin employed this concept in Oakland and had success with it, but it would not be my decision.

If you're on a four-game schedule, you can do wind sprints and work out in between starts, with your big workout in the middle day of the schedule. If you're on a five-game schedule, then your workout can be every other day, but not the day before. Never swim before you pitch a ball game. If you do, be sure you go out and warm up and throw for fifteen or twenty minutes before you rest and pitch. This is true even in Little League.

Defining the Ace

The ace of the pitching staff is the one who is both the most successful and the most intuitive. He knows the hitters in the league better than anyone on his team. He has leadership qualities and is the type of person who is willing to work a little harder, pitch a little longer, and accept the role as the leader of the pitching staff. He also probably has the best pitches.

If the fellow is on his way to the Hall of Fame, then he'll be an ace for many years. The ace is also the physical education leader, and he is the one—along with the pitching coach—who helps the pitchers and makes sure that they work out and are in good condition.

The ace is the pitcher who can hold a 1–0 lead in the seventh inning and then reach in for that little extra adrenaline and finish the ball game, earning both the victory and the credit for a complete game. That's the ace!

Life on the Road as a Player

Years ago, we traveled by train, and there was a certain closeness that became lost with the jet age. The Pullman cars had dining cars, and players could mingle with each other and with reporters on the train and just talk baseball. We'd replay the last game in our minds and discuss previous games. Nowadays the music can be so loud in the clubhouses that you can't even hear yourself think, much less talk to your teammates. In early 2000, under manager Charlie Manual, the Indians put a stop to loud music in the clubhouse.

I preferred train travel to jet travel because it was a better avenue to get acquainted with your teammates on a nonbaseball level. Years ago, we wore shirts and ties, and the Japanese even made their players wear shirts and ties at one point in time. Now our players have a hard time dressing appropriately at all.

I used road trips to further add to my book on the hitters around the league and to better prepare myself for the next start. It was important to me to be as well prepared as possible for the upcoming team, win or lose.

For a player, road trips can be filled with temptation. On the road you must have proper self-discipline. I tell this to all of the players, and the smart ones listen. You have to get your rest. Don't let the hangers-on and free-loaders bother you. Elbow them out of the way. I had that ability, thanks to my father and mother and the values that they instilled in me. I was able to avoid the types of people who I knew would cause trouble.

Life on the road can be a long, lonesome trail if you are not winning. The manager of the ball club must have control. He must have discipline. The only reason they have rules is for those one or two players who don't abide by precepts. Sometimes your best friends can be your worst enemies because they are a big distraction for you. There are also people who want to bask in your glory, distractions you must avoid.

Life on the road can also be terrific and uplifting if you are winning, and if you stay positive, keep to your values, and do not take leave of your common sense.

Today's Sports Agents: Are They Good for the Game?

I never had a sports agent as a young player. My general manager was the scout who had signed me, Cy Slapnicka, and he taught me much about the game in the front office. Cy gave me an invaluable education about the economics of baseball that I carry with me to this day.

Are sports agents good for the game? Some are and some aren't. I wouldn't want an agent. I never had one. I would have my salary based on the number of games I won. That was the arrangement I had with Cleveland. I won more than fifteen games many times, and my salary was adjusted based on the number of fans the ball club drew. I thought my contract was motivating. Today, I have agents who book personal appearances for me.

Sports agents may be necessary for the game because there are so many inexperienced athletes who don't know their market value.

The Autograph

The autograph is sought after, prized, and even sold by ballplayers and fans alike, thus falling within my definition of a commodity. To me, an autograph can either be given away or withheld. It's your property and it's entirely up to you what you do with it.

I feel it's every player's responsibility to sign autographs for fans free of charge, which I do wherever I go. I tell the stars around the league that if they have time to sign, they should. If they don't, the worst thing they can do is sign one autograph and then refuse everyone else. If they sign for only a few in a crowd, everyone else feels cheated and might view the player as cold and aloof. If they are that pressed for time, they should just apologize to the fans and tell them they have obligations. There is no perfect answer to the autograph question.

Little League

Little League is a great social activity. In my day we didn't have a Little League, but we had youth baseball, summer vacation Bible school baseball, and American Legion ball. Today they have tee ball, rubber ball, coach pitch, kid pitch, Mickey Mantle league, Sandy Koufax league, and many other subdivisions for kids of all ages.

As far as building up ballplayers, I'm still circumspect about it. However, it's great culturally. It keeps kids busy and interested, as long as they don't get too involved in winning. That's a big problem with Little League. The stress on winning in some instances has gotten out of hand. There is too much emphasis on winning at an early age, placed on the team by the coaches. Too many parents use their children to fulfill their egos if they weren't athletes, and they chastise their kids which isn't fair. Let the kids play, and make friends, and have a good time. If they have the ability, it will show, but the main focus should be on allowing the kids to enjoy themselves and the game of baseball. If children associate baseball with parental ridicule, then their interest in the sport will be diminished because no child wants to be yelled at while playing a game!

Fort Wayne, Indiana, has a league that was formed years ago that pays all expenses so kids can play baseball. (It was formed by the late Mr. Mack, CEO of Central Soya, the world's largest soybean processor.) This Wildcat League has only one rule: parents cannot stay to see the game. They drop their children off and pick them up after the game. I like this way of letting the children have fun.

I say let *all* kids play. My rule, when I ran Little League, was that *every kid had to play at least two innings every game and go to bat at least once*. I think many Little League coaches ought to sit up and listen to this advice.

Why Ballplayers Adore the Game of Golf

Baseball players love the game of golf because it is both entertaining and excellent for conditioning. Golf is great for your legs. The walking part of it keeps your joints loose, and the fresh air is good for your general health. Golf is a great game for upper body strength and hand-eye coordination, and that's why baseball players can make excellent scratch golfers. The Major League Baseball Players Alumni Association has raised much money for charity through golf tournaments.

Golf also allows for old acquaintances to reminisce, either at the clubhouse or in the golf carts riding from hole to hole. Golf is a businessman's game and many an important business deal has taken place on the golf course, which is another reason why ballplayers love the game.

I enjoy playing golf. While I was in the navy during World War II, I played with Sam Snead often and got to know him quite well, as he was in the squad I was in charge of training. I tell all of the golf pros, "I promise you one thing. If you don't try and tell me how to play golf, I won't try and tell you how to pitch." I don't want any advice on my game, from holding the club, to driving, to putting. If I wanted to get that good, I would have hired a pro to teach me the game through and through sixty years ago.

I enjoy charity tournaments because they benefit people. Golf is just a way for me to make an appearance, help out a worthy charity, obtain some much-needed exercise, and make new friends.

Of course, you can always say "no" to the question "How about a game of golf?" Such was the case when I asked Rogers Hornsby, the second-best hitter I ever pitched to in my career. I had asked Rogers, when he was playing and coaching for the St. Louis Browns in the late 1930s, to play golf with Jim Hegan, Bob Lemon, Early Wynn, and myself. He said, "No thanks, Bob. When I hit a ball I want someone else to chase it!"

Things You Can't Teach

You can't teach common sense nor can you teach intestinal fortitude. You can't teach self-discipline. If you want to be able to plan ahead, and to succeed in baseball and in life, you have to be self-motivated.

I know that there are former football coaches running around the country making $25,000 for assisting corporations in motivating employees. If I were the head of a corporation, I wouldn't take that tack if I found that anyone in my organization was not the least bit motivated. I'd probably just give the person a pink slip and let him or her go find another job. If a person's best interest is more important to the boss than it is to the employee, then that's the time to shake hands and part company.

When it comes to the game of baseball, people often ask me if there is a pitch you cannot teach a pitcher to throw. The fastball has always been my immediate response. You can't teach somebody how to throw a fastball. It's like trying to teach somebody how to grow hair on a bald head. It can't be done. You can't teach somebody to run fast either. If you were not born with the ability to run fast, you'll never be able to. You'll improve a couple of steps but not enough to make you a premier base stealer. You need to assess your strengths and go with them, rather than trying to run fast or throw hard if you can't.

The curveball, on the other hand, is a pitch that can be taught to most everybody. The slider is another pitch that a pitcher can learn and use effectively on a regular basis. You can teach a pitcher how to use these pitches during a ball game and, if the pitcher is receptive to learning, you can teach him how to better locate his pitches.

You can't teach happiness either. The Constitution of the United States guarantees everybody life, liberty, and the pursuit of happiness, but you are only guaranteed the *pursuit* of happiness, not happiness itself. It's up to you to find it for yourself. Sometimes life is not fair at all, and if you've been blessed with good health, take advantage of it. You can't teach someone to maximize their potential. They have to have that desire on their own. You can't teach a professional athlete to try hard or to take care of his or her body. A professional athlete is just that—a professional athlete. If a professional ballplayer does not have the inner desire or motivation by the very fact that he makes a living—and a great living—at what he loves and that millions cheer for him every day, then no motivational speech will make a difference or reach him.

America's Real Heroes

Real heroes are not athletes. Athletics and real heroes don't go together, except in the vein that an athlete should always maintain his dignity. The real heroes to me are those who served in the military and didn't return home. A real hero could be a Nobel Prize winner, a famous physician, a scientist, a policeman, or a fireman. Heroes are individuals who have done something to save lives. Athletes don't save lives. Athletes seldom put their lives at risk. At best, athletes could be role models in an athletic context.

Many of the signers of the Constitution had horrible deaths and lost everything they had to protect the sovereignty of America, and I wonder if people today would be able to do what they did. They were heroes. They gave up their lives to preserve ours. Ballplayers seldom give up their lives to preserve ideals.

There's nothing glamorous about war. The real heroes of World War II, the real heroes of any war, are the ones who didn't return. The survivors were the lucky ones, the ones who returned, such as myself. We lost more than 405,000 men in action defending our democracy in World War II. That doesn't even compare to how many men the Russians lost, or the British, or all the Allies for that matter. For me, it was an extra traumatic event because my father was dying of brain cancer at the time. I was young, impressionable, and deeply saddened by the casualties of war.

Returning from the navy, my father having passed away when I was only twenty-four-years old, gave me a unique perspective on life. I realized how lucky the living soldiers were to return as heroes. In my heart, I knew that being able to do what I love to do and get paid for it was a blessing. Professional athletes are extremely fortunate in that they are able to play a game and earn a great living in the process. To think that I was being paid to play baseball was something special to me.

I received an honor on March 15, 2000, which deeply touched me. I am now proud to say that I am an honorary member of the Green Berets, in recognition of my work for our troops in the Vietnam War in 1969. General Yarborough, now eighty-eight years old, deserves the credit, along with Colonel "Ret." Aaron Bank, because they were the ones who started the Green Berets in Fayetteville, North Carolina. The ceremony for me took place at Fort Bragg, in North Carolina. There are only a handful of Green Berets in the world, and it fills me with great honor and pride to be one of them.

What the Handshake Used to Mean

The world has changed a lot during my lifetime. The handshake is not much of a contract anymore. Nowadays, in too many cases, attorneys have promoted their profession by not accepting handshakes.

The handshake is a sign that your word is everything. I've had a handshake agreement with the Indians ball club for twenty years, ever since Gabe Paul brought me back to the Indians organization in 1980.

I believe that the handshake is a personification of your character. Your character is always following you like a shadow. You can lose your health and your money, and regain both of them, but once you lose your character, you'll never regain it! It doesn't matter how far you go and how fast you run, you can't outrun your shadow. Your shadow and your character are one, and the meaning of the handshake is the physical embodiment of a person's character and the emphasis that person places on his or her integrity.

My Millennium Wish List for Kids

I wish kids would play fewer games on the Internet and play more sports. Otherwise, we're going to become a nation of couch potatoes, watching television and working on the computer. That is why many players come from the Caribbean, Venezuela, Colombia, Panama, even Australia, the Dominican Republic, Puerto Rico, and down through the islands. American children are not playing baseball that much and one reason is that baseball is not an income sport in high school or college. Society promotes the income sports such as football and basketball, and as a consequence, baseball is getting shortchanged by our educational institutions.

My wish list for kids is that they study hard, eat right, take up athletics, have fun while they're young, and hopefully find a career that embodies what they love doing.

How to Live to Be a Hundred

Nobody knows the secret to the Fountain of Youth; otherwise, everybody would live to be a hundred. Life is not always fair. I often wonder whether it was ever intended to be. Perhaps we'll never know. Luck, fate, and the roll of the dice are very unpredictable. I once heard about a doctor who wrote a book on how to live to a hundred. He didn't make it and the book didn't sell.

Thank You, Baseball, for Everything

Baseball has been very good to me, and I appreciate it. I have made appearances all over the world, from my military tour and playing days through the many years after my playing career ended. I've coached in Japan and appeared at minor league ballparks all over the country, trying to repay the debt I owe this game. Since I retired in 1956, I've visited military bases in England, Germany,

Japan, and elsewhere. I was privileged to visit our troops in Vietnam and try to lend them moral support.

I have established the Bob Feller Museum in Van Meter, Iowa, and visitors come from all over to see artifacts not on display in the Cooperstown Hall of Fame. My son, Steve, designed the museum, making it even more special to me. My wife, Anne, a former lighting specialist with General Electric, helped design the lighting. The museum has personal belongings of mine, rare photographs, candy bar wrappers, balls, bats, caps, uniforms, and contracts. My museum is open seven days a week, except on major holidays, and is located one mile off I-80, eighteen miles west of Des Moines at exit 113. It's a great museum, and the people who run it are conscientious, generous with their time, and great fans of the game of baseball.

I have a wonderful family. I have a wonderful wife, Anne. I also have three wonderful sons: Steve, Marty, and Bruce. Anne has a daughter, Rachel, and a son, John.

I enjoy going to Jacobs Field and mingling with the young kids and the future generation in baseball. Gabe Paul brought me back in 1980, and I was delighted he did so. Anne and I have attended games ever since. I usually sit in the press box during the games. If I sit in the grandstand, fans will come over to me and stand there and talk, and people behind me have complained that their view is blocked. By not showing up in the grandstand, I don't bother any fans.

I have tried to be good for baseball. I go to Cooperstown every year at Induction Weekend and try to sign autographs and shake hands with the many fans. I also enjoy talking to youngsters in schools and giving them hope for the future.

Feller Family Sayings

I hope these sayings will entertain, inspire, and enlighten all of the readers of this book. My dad used to recite these adages to me and they are part of the Feller family ideology.

- A man convinced against his will is of the same opinion still.
- You can only be young once, but immature forever.
- The less you say, the longer it will take people to find out how little you know.
- An hour of sleep before midnight is worth two hours of sleep after midnight.
- The best way to judge the future is to know what has happened in the past.
- Every day is a different day. You can have a bad day and wake up the next day and have a great day.
- Lost time is never found. You're put here on Earth for a given amount of time, and what you do

during the time that the good Lord has given you says much about you. It's your legacy.

- It is useless for the sheep to pass a resolution in favor of vegetarianism while the wolf remains of a different opinion.
- Every generation makes the same mistakes and you can't tell them differently. They have to make the mistakes themselves and then find out others were right.
- The man who knows how will always have a job working for the man who knows why.
- When playing the stock market, make your move before the rumor is proved true or false.
- There are no atheists in foxholes.
- Military leaders, CEOs, and other leaders of industry can only command 90 percent of a person's ability. The last 10 percent must be given willingly by the individual, and that 10 percent is the difference between winning or losing a battle and success or failure in life.
- Sometimes it's better to be lucky than good.
- You can fool most of the people all the time and part of the people some of the time, but you cannot fool all of the people all of the time.
- You can lose your money or your health and regain them, but you'll never regain your character if you lose it.
- Character is like your shadow—it follows you wherever you go.